SHE RISES
S T U D I O S

**THE FEMALE
FINANCIAL ROADMAP**
NAVIGATE TO WEALTH WITH CONFIDENCE

FEMALE MONEY
Playbook

HANNA OLIVAS & ADRIANA LUNA CARLOS
HANNA AND ADRIANA ALONG WITH 8 AUTHORS

Table of Contents

INTRODUCTION

Welcome to the "Female Money Playbook" – a groundbreaking guide tailored for the modern woman ready to conquer her financial future with confidence and finesse. In the pages that follow, you'll embark on an empowering journey that unveils the financial strategies employed by some of the most successful women in the world.

In a landscape where financial literacy remains a crucial skill, this playbook serves as your trusted companion, offering a comprehensive roadmap to navigate the intricate terrain of finance. Whether you're a seasoned investor or just beginning to explore the world of wealth-building, you'll find invaluable insights and practical advice to propel you towards your financial goals.

From investment tips that demystify the complexities of the stock market to wealth-building strategies designed to secure your financial freedom, each chapter is meticulously crafted to equip you with the knowledge and tools needed to take control of your financial destiny.

But this book is more than just a guide – it's a call to action. It's a reminder that financial independence is not just a dream reserved for the few, but a tangible reality within reach for every woman willing to seize it. Through stories of perseverance, resilience, and triumph, you'll discover that the path to success is not always linear, but with determination and strategic planning, it is always achievable.

So, whether you're aiming to grow your investments, start your own business, or simply gain a better understanding of your financial landscape, the "Female Money Playbook" is here to empower you every step of the way. Get ready to unleash your financial potential and embark on a journey towards lasting prosperity and success.

Hanna Olivas

Founder and CEO of She Rises Studios

https://www.linkedin.com/company/she-rises-studios/
https://www.facebook.com/sherisesstudios
https://www.instagram.com/sherisesstudios_llc/
www.SheRisesStudios.com

Author, Speaker, and Founder. Hanna was born and raised in Las Vegas, Nevada, and has paved her way to becoming one of the most influential women of 2022. Hanna is the co-founder of She Rises Studios and the founder of the Brave & Beautiful Blood Cancer Foundation. Her journey started in 2017 when she was first diagnosed with Multiple Myeloma, an incurable blood cancer. Now more than ever, her focus is to empower other women to become leaders because The Future is Female. She is currently traveling and speaking publicly to women to educate them on entrepreneurship, leadership, and owning the female power within.

FROM HUMBLE BEGINNINGS TO SEVEN-FIGURE SUCCESS: MY JOURNEY AS A FEMALE MONEY MAKER

By Hanna Olivas

Introduction

Growing up, I never imagined that I would become a successful entrepreneur, let alone a female money maker in the women's entrepreneurship space. My journey is rooted in humble beginnings, raised by a single mother and grandparents who didn't graduate high school. Despite the odds, I now own several businesses generating seven-figure incomes. Along the way, I've faced significant challenges, including a diagnosis of multiple myeloma, raising five children, and balancing roles as a wife and grandmother. This story is not just about my achievements but also about the importance of empowering women to become financial powerhouses. In this chapter, I'll share my personal journey and offer 40 key steps and strategies to grow a seven-figure income and manage it effectively.

My Early Years: Foundations of Resilience

The Influence of My Single Mother and Grandparents

My single mother and grandparents were my first role models in resilience and perseverance. They worked tirelessly to provide for our family, teaching me the value of hard work and determination. Despite their lack of formal education, they instilled in me a strong belief in the power of self-reliance and entrepreneurship.

Growing up in a household where every dollar counted, I witnessed firsthand the sacrifices my mother and grandparents made to ensure we had what we needed. My grandfather worked multiple jobs, and my grandmother took in laundry and sewing work to make ends meet. My mother juggled various part-time jobs while attending night school to improve her prospects. Their unwavering dedication and relentless work ethic were lessons I absorbed deeply.

Overcoming Early Challenges

Living in an environment where financial stability was always a concern taught me invaluable lessons about managing money and finding creative solutions to problems. From a young age, I learned to be resourceful and think outside the box. When other kids were playing, I was brainstorming ways to earn a little extra money, whether it was selling homemade crafts or offering to run errands for neighbors.

These early experiences laid the groundwork for my future success as an entrepreneur. They taught me that success is not handed to you; it is earned through hard work, determination, and a willingness to face and overcome challenges. This mindset became a cornerstone of my entrepreneurial journey.

Breaking Barriers: The Path to Entrepreneurship

Starting My First Business

My entrepreneurial journey began with a small business idea. I started with minimal resources but a lot of passion and determination. My first venture was a modest online retail business, selling handmade jewelry and accessories. I worked from my kitchen table, using every spare moment to create products, manage orders, and market my business.

I quickly realized that the key to success was not just having a great idea but also having the tenacity to see it through. I faced numerous obstacles, from supply chain issues to marketing challenges. But each problem presented an opportunity to learn and grow. I attended local business workshops, networked with other entrepreneurs, and immersed myself in books and articles about business management and marketing.

Learning from Failures

Like many entrepreneurs, I faced my fair share of failures. There were times when sales were low, and I doubted whether I could make my business work. I remember the first time I invested a significant amount of money in a marketing campaign that yielded almost no results. It was a tough pill to swallow, but it taught me invaluable lessons about understanding my market and the importance of testing strategies on a smaller scale before committing substantial resources.

Each setback was a learning opportunity, teaching me valuable lessons about resilience, adaptability, and the importance of perseverance. I learned to view failures not as the end of the road but as stepping stones to success. They were opportunities to refine my strategies, improve my products, and better understand my customers.

Building a Diverse Portfolio

Over time, I diversified my business interests, expanding into various industries. This diversification not only mitigated risks but also opened up new revenue streams, contributing to my seven-figure income. I ventured into areas such as real estate, consultancy, and e-commerce, each with its unique challenges and rewards.

Diversifying my portfolio was a strategic decision. It allowed me to leverage my strengths in different markets and spread my risks. For instance, while my e-commerce business provided steady income, real estate investments offered long-term growth and stability. Consultancy, on the other hand, allowed me to share my knowledge and experience with other aspiring entrepreneurs, creating a fulfilling and profitable venture.

The Role of Personal Challenges

Managing Multiple Myeloma

Being diagnosed with multiple myeloma was a life-changing event. The news was devastating, and the treatment process was grueling. However, I refused to let it define me or limit my potential. I managed my health with the same determination I applied to my businesses, proving that it's possible to thrive even in the face of adversity.

I adopted a holistic approach to my health, combining medical treatments with a focus on nutrition, exercise, and mental well-being. I sought support from my family, friends, and a network of fellow cancer patients who provided invaluable encouragement and advice. This experience taught me the importance of resilience and the power of a positive mindset.

Balancing Family and Business

Raising five children while running multiple businesses required exceptional time management and prioritization skills. My family has always been my greatest source of strength and motivation, driving me to succeed not just for myself but for them as well.

Balancing family and business was not easy. There were countless late nights and early mornings, juggling school runs, business meetings, and everything in between. But my family was my anchor, and their support and understanding were crucial. I learned to prioritize my time, delegate responsibilities, and create systems that allowed me to be present both at home and in my business.

Empowering Women: The Importance of Financial Independence

Overcoming the Fear of Money

One of the most significant barriers women face in entrepreneurship is the fear of money. It's essential to break this stigma and embrace the concept of financial independence. Money is a tool that can empower women to achieve their dreams and create lasting impact.

I have encountered many women who shy away from discussing finances or pursuing financial goals, often due to societal conditioning or lack of confidence. It's crucial to change this narrative. Financial independence is not just about accumulating wealth; it's about having the freedom and security to make choices that align with your values and aspirations.

The Need for Female Role Models

Having female role models in the entrepreneurial space is crucial. Women need to see others like themselves succeeding, breaking barriers, and achieving financial independence. It creates a sense of possibility and inspires others to pursue their entrepreneurial dreams.

Throughout my journey, I have been fortunate to connect with incredible women who have inspired and mentored me. Their stories of resilience, innovation, and success have been a constant source of motivation. As I continue to grow my businesses and achieve new milestones, I am committed to paying it forward by mentoring and supporting other women on their entrepreneurial journeys.

40 Key Steps and Strategies to Grow a Seven-Figure Income

1. Believe in Yourself

Confidence is the foundation of success. Believe in your abilities and your vision.

Believing in yourself is not just a motivational slogan; it's a critical factor in achieving entrepreneurial success. Self-confidence allows you to take risks, make bold decisions, and persevere in the face of challenges. It's about trusting your instincts and having faith in your abilities.

2. Set Clear Goals

Define your long-term and short-term goals. Having a clear roadmap helps you stay focused and motivated.

Goal setting is an essential part of any successful business strategy. Break down your long-term vision into achievable short-term goals. This approach not only keeps you focused but also provides a sense of accomplishment as you achieve each milestone.

3. Continuous Learning

Invest in your education. Attend workshops, read books, and stay updated with industry trends.

The business landscape is constantly evolving, and staying informed is crucial. Continuously seek opportunities to learn and grow. Attend industry conferences, enroll in online courses, and read widely to stay ahead of the curve.

4. Network Effectively

Build a strong network of mentors, peers, and industry experts. Networking opens up opportunities and provides valuable support.

Networking is more than just exchanging business cards; it's about building meaningful relationships. Engage with mentors who can provide guidance, peers who can share experiences, and industry experts who can offer insights. Networking can lead to new opportunities, partnerships, and collaborations.

5. Leverage Technology

Use technology to streamline operations, reach a broader audience, and improve efficiency.

Technology is a powerful tool for business growth. Utilize digital marketing, e-commerce platforms, and automation tools to enhance your operations. Stay updated with the latest technological advancements to stay competitive.

6. Diversify Income Streams

Don't rely on a single source of income. Explore multiple revenue streams to mitigate risks.

Diversifying your income streams reduces risk and increases financial stability. Consider expanding into complementary markets or developing new products and services. Diversification can help you weather economic downturns and seize new opportunities.

7. Financial Literacy

Educate yourself about finances. Understand budgeting, investing, and financial planning.

Financial literacy is a critical skill for any entrepreneur. Understand your financial statements, learn about investment options, and develop a solid financial plan. Being financially savvy allows you to make informed decisions and grow your wealth.

8. Invest Wisely

Make informed investment decisions. Diversify your investments to grow your wealth.

Investing is not just about making money; it's about making your money work for you. Diversify your investments across different asset classes to spread risk. Research thoroughly before making investment decisions to ensure they align with your financial goals.

9. Build a Strong Team

Surround yourself with talented and dedicated individuals who share your vision.

A strong team is the backbone of any successful business. Hire individuals who complement your skills and share your vision. Invest in their development and create a positive work environment that fosters collaboration and innovation.

10. Delegate Responsibilities

Learn to delegate tasks to focus on strategic decisions and growth.

Delegation is essential for scaling your business. Trust your team to handle operational tasks, allowing you to focus on strategic decisions and growth initiatives. Effective delegation empowers your team and enhances productivity.

11. Adaptability

Be flexible and adaptable to changing market conditions and opportunities.

The ability to adapt to changing circumstances is a key trait of successful entrepreneurs. Stay informed about market trends, be open to new ideas, and be willing to pivot your strategies when necessary.

12. Customer Focus

Prioritize customer satisfaction. Happy customers are loyal customers.

Customer satisfaction is the cornerstone of a successful business. Listen to your customers, understand their needs, and deliver exceptional service. Happy customers are more likely to become repeat buyers and brand advocates.

13. Innovation

Stay ahead of the curve by continuously innovating and improving your products or services.

Innovation drives growth and keeps your business competitive. Continuously seek ways to improve your products, services, and processes. Encourage creativity within your team and be open to new ideas.

14. Brand Building

Invest in building a strong brand that resonates with your target audience.

A strong brand sets you apart from the competition and builds customer loyalty. Invest in branding efforts, including your logo, messaging, and customer experience. Ensure your brand reflects your values and resonates with your target audience.

15. Marketing Strategies

Develop effective marketing strategies to reach and engage your audience.

Effective marketing is essential for attracting and retaining customers. Develop a comprehensive marketing plan that includes digital marketing, social media, content marketing, and traditional advertising. Tailor your strategies to reach and engage your target audience.

16. Time Management

Master the art of time management to balance various aspects of your life and business.

Time management is crucial for maintaining productivity and achieving a healthy work-life balance. Prioritize tasks, set realistic deadlines, and eliminate distractions. Use tools and techniques such as time blocking and to-do lists to manage your time effectively.

17. Health and Well-being

Prioritize your health and well-being. A healthy entrepreneur is a productive entrepreneur.

Your health is your most valuable asset. Prioritize physical activity, a balanced diet, and adequate rest. Manage stress through mindfulness practices, hobbies, and spending time with loved ones. A healthy lifestyle enhances productivity and resilience.

18. Risk Management

Identify and mitigate risks to protect your business and personal assets.

Risk management is essential for business stability. Identify potential risks, develop contingency plans, and take proactive measures to mitigate them. Regularly review and update your risk management strategies to address new challenges.

19. Legal Considerations

Ensure your business complies with all legal requirements and protections.

Legal compliance is critical for protecting your business. Understand the legal requirements for your industry, obtain necessary licenses and permits, and adhere to regulations. Consult with legal professionals to ensure your business is protected.

20. Financial Planning

Create a robust financial plan that includes savings, investments, and emergency funds.

A comprehensive financial plan provides a roadmap for achieving your financial goals. Include short-term and long-term savings, investment strategies, and an emergency fund. Regularly review and adjust your financial plan to stay on track.

21. Customer Feedback

Use customer feedback to improve and refine your products or services.

Customer feedback is invaluable for continuous improvement. Actively seek feedback through surveys, reviews, and direct interactions. Use the insights to enhance your products, services, and customer experience.

22. Sales Strategies

Develop effective sales strategies to drive revenue growth.

Sales strategies are crucial for business growth. Develop a clear sales process, set achievable targets, and track performance. Train your sales team to effectively communicate your value proposition and close deals.

23. Expense Management

Keep a close eye on your expenses and reduce unnecessary costs.

Effective expense management is essential for maintaining profitability. Regularly review your expenses, identify areas for cost savings, and implement efficient processes. Avoid unnecessary expenditures and invest in value-added activities.

24. Quality Control

Maintain high-quality standards in your products or services.

Quality control is critical for customer satisfaction and brand reputation. Implement rigorous quality control processes to ensure consistency and excellence. Address quality issues promptly to maintain customer trust.

25. Vision and Mission

Define your vision and mission to guide your business decisions and strategies.

A clear vision and mission provide direction and purpose. Define your long-term goals and the impact you want to achieve. Use your vision and mission to guide your business decisions and align your team.

26. Mentorship

Seek mentorship from experienced entrepreneurs to gain insights and guidance.

Mentorship provides valuable support and guidance. Connect with experienced entrepreneurs who can offer insights, share their experiences, and provide advice. A mentor can help you navigate challenges and accelerate your growth.

27. Work-Life Balance

Strive for a healthy work-life balance to avoid burnout and maintain productivity.

Maintaining a work-life balance is essential for long-term success. Set boundaries, prioritize self-care, and make time for family and personal activities. A balanced lifestyle enhances productivity and well-being.

28. Customer Relationships

Build strong relationships with your customers to foster loyalty and trust.

Building strong customer relationships is key to retention and growth. Engage with your customers, understand their needs, and provide personalized experiences. Strong relationships foster loyalty and positive word-of-mouth.

29. Scalability

Design your business model to be scalable for future growth.

Scalability is crucial for expanding your business. Design your operations, processes, and systems to support growth. Plan for scalability from the outset to ensure smooth and sustainable expansion.

30. Data-Driven Decisions

Use data and analytics to make informed business decisions.

Data-driven decisions enhance accuracy and effectiveness. Collect and analyze data on your operations, customers, and market trends. Use the insights to inform your strategies and improve performance.

31. Negotiation Skills

Develop strong negotiation skills to secure better deals and partnerships.

Negotiation skills are essential for securing favorable terms and partnerships. Prepare thoroughly, understand your counterpart's interests, and communicate your value. Effective negotiation leads to win-win outcomes.

32. Community Engagement

Engage with your community and give back to create a positive impact.

Community engagement builds goodwill and enhances your brand reputation. Participate in local events, support community initiatives, and contribute to causes that align with your values. Giving back creates a positive impact and strengthens your connections.

33. Sustainability

Incorporate sustainable practices to ensure long-term success.

Sustainability is increasingly important for business success. Implement environmentally friendly practices, reduce waste, and support sustainable initiatives. Sustainability enhances your brand and appeals to conscious consumers.

34. Personal Development

Invest in your personal development to enhance your leadership and entrepreneurial skills.

Personal development is a continuous journey. Seek opportunities to improve your skills, knowledge, and mindset. Personal growth enhances your leadership abilities and contributes to your business success.

35. Stay Persistent

Persistence is key to overcoming challenges and achieving success.

Persistence is essential for navigating the ups and downs of entrepreneurship. Stay committed to your goals, maintain a positive attitude, and keep pushing forward. Persistence turns challenges into opportunities for growth.

36. Embrace Failure

View failures as learning opportunities and stepping stones to success.

Failure is a natural part of the entrepreneurial journey. Embrace failures as valuable learning experiences. Analyze what went wrong, identify lessons, and use the insights to improve and innovate.

37. Customer Retention

Focus on retaining existing customers through excellent service and engagement.

Customer retention is crucial for sustained growth. Provide exceptional service, engage with your customers, and reward loyalty. Retaining customers is more cost-effective than acquiring new ones and leads to long-term success.

38. Market Research

Conduct thorough market research to understand your industry and target audience.

Market research provides critical insights into your industry and customers. Conduct regular research to understand market trends, customer preferences, and competitive dynamics. Use the insights to inform your strategies and stay ahead of the competition.

39. Strategic Partnerships

Form strategic partnerships to expand your reach and capabilities.

Strategic partnerships enhance your capabilities and reach. Identify potential partners who complement your strengths and share your vision. Collaborate on initiatives that create mutual value and drive growth.

40. Celebrate Successes

Take time to celebrate your successes and milestones to stay motivated.

Celebrating successes is important for maintaining motivation and morale. Acknowledge your achievements, reward your team, and reflect on your progress. Celebrations create a positive work environment and reinforce your commitment to your goals.

Conclusion

My journey from humble beginnings to becoming a female money maker in the women entrepreneurship space is a testament to the power of resilience, determination, and continuous learning. It's essential for women to overcome the fear of money and embrace financial independence. By following the steps and strategies outlined above, you can grow a seven-figure income and manage it effectively. Remember, success is not just about achieving financial goals but also about creating a positive impact and inspiring others to pursue their entrepreneurial dreams. Let's continue to empower and uplift each other as we break barriers and redefine success in the world of entrepreneurship.

Final Thoughts

As you embark on your entrepreneurial journey, remember that success is a marathon, not a sprint. There will be challenges, setbacks, and moments of doubt, but each obstacle is an opportunity to learn and grow.

Adriana Luna Carlos

Founder and CEO of She Rises Studios & FENIX TV

https://www.linkedin.com/in/adriana-luna-carlos/
https://www.facebook.com/adrianalunacarlos
https://www.instagram.com/sherisesstudios_llc/
https://www.sherisesstudios.com/
https://www.srslatina.com/
https://fenixtv.app/

Adriana Luna Carlos is an accomplished web and graphic designer, author, and mentor with a passion for helping women succeed in life and business. With over 10 years of experience in graphic and web arts, Adriana has built a reputation as an innovative leader and entrepreneur. In 2020, she co-founded She Rises Studios, a multi-digital media company and publishing house that has helped countless clients achieve their branding and marketing goals. In 2023, she co-created FENIX TV, an online streaming platform that showcases stories of people breaking barriers, shattering stereotypes, and triumphing against the odds.

As an advocate for women's success, Adriana challenges her clients and mentees to strive for nothing less than excellence. She has a deep understanding of the insecurities and challenges that women often face in the business world and provides the guidance and resources needed to overcome them. Her success as a business leader and entrepreneur has made her a sought-after mentor and speaker at events around the world.

Through her work, Adriana has demonstrated a commitment to creating opportunities for women to succeed in business and life. Her passion for innovation, leadership, and women's empowerment has made her a respected figure in the business community, and her impact will undoubtedly continue to inspire and empower women for years to come.

MY DNA OF BECOMING AN ENTREPRENEUR

By Adriana Luna Carlos

Looking back at my journey, I realize how early lessons about money and resilience shaped my path in entrepreneurship. Growing up in a family where entrepreneurship runs deep, I felt like it was in my DNA to become an entrepreneur. My family's experiences taught me invaluable lessons in managing finances wisely and staying strong during tough times. These lessons weren't just about theory; they were about real-life skills that guided me as I started my own business.

One of the biggest challenges I faced early on was balancing big dreams with practical realities. Dreaming big is important, but turning those dreams into reality takes hard work and smart decisions. Being an entrepreneur is more than just starting and running a business; it's a journey that changes who you are and how you look at the world. When you decide to become an entrepreneur, you're jumping into a world full of challenges and chances to grow.

Early Beginnings I always think that I stumbled into something amazing when I went to sign up for the Graphics Communication Academy (GCA). I knew some of what we would potentially get into, but what I didn't know was how much it would change the trajectory of my life and how many new doors it would open. At that time, I loved computers but was still such a novice. The prospect of using those "new" Apple computers was thrilling. This is where my love for Apple would grow. I went in with a friend as she signed up for the Visual Arts & Design Academy (VADA), but I knew I couldn't draw at all. So, I leaped and went into a program where I felt I belonged more, even though it meant I wouldn't know anyone. This was a commitment because it was a three-year program at my high school. Most teenagers barely know what they want to eat, let alone make a three-year commitment so rashly. But this is who I was and who I am. I've always been someone who dives into the deep end without fearing the "what ifs." I was excited to overcome obstacles because I loved a challenge.

One of my favorite experiences was getting to design a logo and card for a previous alumni reunion. It was either their 40th or 50th reunion, and a group of elderly alumni came into our class. They looked so amazed and excited to see our class and to know what the future had turned into. I remember feeling so lucky to be a part of their history. I was second in this "competition"; they ended up selecting another design, but this only fueled me more! My teacher was pretty cool. She always showed us her artwork from projects outside of class to give us a glimpse of "real-world experiences." She didn't treat us like students; she treated us as colleagues. We got to do fun projects that mixed design with a sense of ownership and entrepreneurship. She taught us how to make products like t-shirts, school newspapers, and even how to create pitches, websites, resumes, and cover letters. It was a future entrepreneur's dream. I felt so at home and inspired daily.

Taking the Leap I was motivated to start my own design business at 18 because I noticed how people were hiring graphic designers at astronomical rates for work that often looked subpar. I wanted to show myself that I could rise to the challenge, make some side money in college, and be independent. The idea was thrilling at the time. I began by placing ads on Craigslist, offering services for logo design, brochures, flyers, and business cards. My prices were low since I was still fresh in the field. This venture taught me how to communicate with strangers, negotiate deals, and market my skills realistically while still exuding confidence. It was scary but also incredibly fun! However, I faced significant challenges. Many customers doubted my abilities due to my age and gender. Some tried to take advantage of me, assuming I would back down easily. But I always stood my ground and let my work speak for itself. Navigating Challenges Handling financial challenges and resource constraints was one of the biggest hurdles. I had limited funds and no formal business training.

I had to learn everything on the fly—how to budget, manage time, and balance my personal life with the demands of running a business. There were moments of doubt and fear, but I pushed through by focusing on my passion for design and the satisfaction of delivering quality work. One particular challenge was balancing college coursework with client deadlines. There were nights when I barely slept, juggling design projects and studying for exams. But each completed project and satisfied client reinforced my belief in my capabilities and motivated me to keep going.

Successes and Milestones Despite the challenges, there were many early successes that validated my efforts. One of my first big breaks came when a local restaurant hired me to design their entire branding package. Seeing my designs come to life in menus, signage, and advertisements around town was immensely rewarding.

As you deal with these ups and downs, you start to learn a lot about yourself. You figure out what your true strengths and weaknesses are and what really drives you. This journey makes you more aware of who you are and gives you confidence, which is important in both your business and personal life.

Running your own business is empowering. You're in control of your own destiny, making decisions that shape your future. This control is incredibly rewarding and motivates you to keep pushing towards your dreams. Your journey can inspire others to take control of their lives and chase their own dreams too.

Every day as an entrepreneur is a chance to learn something new. You pick up skills like managing money, marketing, and leading people. This constant learning makes you adaptable and ready for anything. It helps you become better at solving problems and communicating with others, which is useful in all parts of life.

Being an entrepreneur also means you get to be creative and innovative. You get to think of new ideas and bring them to life. Whether it's developing a new product or finding better ways to do things, this creativity keeps you excited and engaged. It also inspires others to think creatively.

Practical Steps to Empower Your Entrepreneurial Journey

Starting a business is an exciting adventure filled with lots of ups and downs. As women, we sometimes face extra challenges, but with the right tools and mindset, we can tackle anything that comes our way. In this chapter, I'll share some practical steps that can help you navigate your entrepreneurial path with confidence and purpose.

Step 1: Crafting Your Unique Value Proposition

Your unique value proposition (UVP) is what makes your business stand out. It's that special something that you offer and why people should choose you over others. Figuring out your UVP is super important because it shapes everything you do in your business, from marketing to how you connect with customers.

Start by getting to know your audience really well. Who are they? What do they need? Spend time researching and talking to potential customers to understand their likes, dislikes, and pain points. This will help you tailor your products or services to meet their needs in a way that nobody else does.

For example, if you're starting a skincare line, your UVP could be that you use only natural ingredients and promote sustainable practices. Talk about how your brand not only offers great products but also cares about the environment. This approach attracts customers who share your values and helps you stand out in the crowded beauty market.

Step 2: Building a Strong Personal and Professional Network

Networking is like having a superpower in the business world. It opens doors to new opportunities, gives you valuable advice, and connects you with people who can support you on your journey. Building a strong network takes effort, but it's totally worth it.

Start by finding events, workshops, and online groups related to your industry. Go to these places with an open mind and a willingness to meet new people. Don't be shy to introduce yourself and share your passion. Networking isn't just about what others can do for you; it's also about what you can offer them. Approach every conversation with the idea of helping each other out.

Online platforms like LinkedIn are also great for expanding your network. Join groups and participate in discussions about your field. Share your knowledge, ask questions, and connect with people who share your interests. Building a strong online presence can complement your in-person efforts and help you reach a wider audience.

Step 3: Developing Financial Literacy and Savvy

Understanding money is a must for any successful entrepreneur. Knowing how to manage your finances and make smart investments is key to growing your business. Many women entrepreneurs find it hard to access capital and manage cash flow, so getting good at financial stuff is really important.

Start by learning the basics of financial management. There are tons of free resources out there, like online courses, webinars, and podcasts, that can help you understand things like budgeting and financial planning. Books and blogs about finance can also be really helpful.

Once you have a handle on the basics, create a solid financial plan for your business. Make a budget that outlines your income, expenses, and financial goals. Keep an eye on your finances regularly to see how you're doing and make adjustments as needed. If you're not sure about something, don't be afraid to ask for help from a financial advisor or accountant.

Step 4: Leveraging Technology to Streamline Operations

Technology can make running a business so much easier. It can help you get things done faster, keep track of everything, and stay connected with your customers. Using the right tools and platforms can give you a big advantage and free up your time to focus on growing your business.

Look at different parts of your business and see where technology can help. For example, customer relationship management (CRM) software can help you keep track of your customers and sales. Project management tools can help you organize your work and keep your team on the same page.

Having a strong online presence is also super important. Make sure your website is easy to use and shows up in search results. Use social media to connect with your audience and build a community around your brand. Email marketing tools can help you keep in touch with your customers and let them know about new products or services.

Step 5: Cultivating a Growth Mindset

Having a growth mindset means believing that you can always learn and improve. This mindset is crucial for entrepreneurs because it helps you stay positive, keep learning, and tackle challenges head-on.

Start by seeing failure as a chance to learn. Instead of thinking of setbacks as failures, view them as valuable lessons that help you grow. Celebrate your progress, no matter how small, and always look for ways to improve.

Surround yourself with positive influences that encourage this mindset. Connect with mentors, peers, and communities that inspire you to keep pushing forward. Ask for feedback and use it to get better at what you do. Remember, entrepreneurship is a long journey, and every experience helps you get better and stronger.

Step 6: Prioritizing Self-Care and Well-Being

Running a business can be really demanding, and it's easy to get caught up in the hustle and forget about taking care of yourself. But balancing work and self-care is super important for long-term success and happiness.

Make your health a priority by staying active, eating well, and getting enough sleep. These habits boost your energy, improve your mood, and help you handle stress better. Practices like meditation or yoga can help you stay calm and focused.

Set boundaries to make sure you have time to relax and do things you enjoy. Whether it's spending time with friends and family, pursuing hobbies, or just taking a break, these moments are crucial for recharging and staying passionate about your work.

Embracing Your Empowered Journey

Becoming an entrepreneur isn't just about starting a business—it's a path of learning and growth. As entrepreneurs, we face challenges that test our resolve. Each setback isn't a roadblock but a chance to learn and improve. It's about bouncing back stronger, whether it's overcoming financial hurdles or adapting our strategies.

Beyond personal growth, entrepreneurship is about making a difference. It's about building connections with our team, customers, and fellow entrepreneurs, creating a positive impact in our communities.

Continual learning and innovation drive our journey forward. Whether it's developing new ideas or improving our business practices, each step brings us closer to our goals.

Remember, your journey is unique. Embrace each challenge with confidence, knowing that every lesson learned and every milestone achieved shapes your success. By staying resilient, fostering relationships, and embracing innovation, you can turn your dreams into reality and inspire others along the way.

Heather Stokes Benton

Founder, Owner and CEO of Financial GPS

https://www.linkedin.com/in/heather-stokes-899624204/
https://www.facebook.com/HeatherStokesGetFinanciallyFit
https://www.instagram.com/heathersfinancialfocus/
https://www.facebook.com/groups/490021218981192

I am a wife, mother, homeschooler, and business owner. I am a giver, a motivator, and a developer, and I do not accept the answer no. I only see it as a challenge. My road to success has changed many times. Life has derailed my journey, and I have built a new path each time. I went to college for Forensic Psychology and worked for multiple government agencies over the next eight years. When I met my husband, he was a flight attendant and owned a limousine business. We lived a lavish life. 9/11 was our first major setback; three years later, he suffered a major injury and pancreatic cancer at 40. I could have given up, but with three girls depending on us, that was not an option. I had to learn how to be creative with money. Now it is my mission to help others to go from surviving to thriving. Being a mother and running a business can feel overwhelming at times. I find the key to keeping it all together is balance.

IT'S OUR MONEY IN THE MODERN WORLD

By Heather Stokes Benton

We have heard them say in songs, "I got mind on my money and money on my mind"—how sadly true that is. A number of studies have demonstrated a cyclical link between financial worries and mental health problems such as depression, anxiety, and substance abuse. Financial problems adversely impact your mental health. The stress of debt and other financial issues can leave you feeling depressed. An individual's financial well-being is one of the greatest indicators of their mental wellness. A study published in 2011 by the peer-reviewed medical journal JAMA Psychiatry compared the mental health of those making under $20,000 per year to those making over $70,000 per year. This research showed that low levels of household income are associated with several lifetime mental disorders and suicide attempts. The study also showed that a reduction in household income is associated with an increased risk of incident mental health disorders, substance abuse, and loss of sleep, even causing changes in physical health.

How does money affect our mental health, and is it significant? In short, yes! It is very important, now more than ever, given the economic landscape caused by COVID-19. Money is arguably the single most important factor for civilizing the modern world. The invention of money established the consenting relationships between buyers and sellers, but also workers and owners. This medium of exchange is understood across the globe and is the foundation of our society. These small pieces of paper dictate almost every aspect of our lives; perhaps most importantly, our mental health and stability. So, the questions are: How can we change our relationship with money? How can we start positive habits and rewrite our financial wellness?

Many people view money as dirty, negative, even evil. I have found that most of the time these unhealthy views on money are due to generational trauma, historical standards, and gender inequality. What I found is that, for many of us, there is trauma associated with finances—trauma that has been carried through many generations.

We talk about the effects of historical trauma related to oppression and being marginalized. The intense emotions that come with financial struggles, however, are rarely mentioned. The shame, guilt, feeling of being gaslighted by your own bank account, memory loss regarding spending, paranoia that you were overcharged, and mistrust that you are underpaid are all part of the constant stress about money for so many women.

Women have increasingly become the sole providers for our households. We have obtained the highest rates of education and are progressively landing more management and leadership positions. Even in cases where men are the main household providers, women still play a vital role in making key decisions about how the money is spent.

However, there have been fierce and sudden changes in family structure caused by a history of patriarchy and white supremacy. Men continue to be torn from their families—lynched, imprisoned, and deported—leaving women to deal with the aftermath. Most women have never been taught to be confident with money.

There are so many unconscious ideas embedded in our relationship to money, generally tied to our sense of worth and value, and associated with crisis. Financial trauma is pervasive, yet largely unaddressed. The first step toward financial stability and wellness is identifying your relationship with money and what needs to change in your mindset. Understanding money is a tool we need, and it's within our control.

Let's shift gears and talk about controlling, managing, and growing our money so we can sleep at night, have less stress, and better overall wellness. I am going to give you six step cure to money management to get you started on your path to financial wellness.

1. Get Organized: List all your fixed and variable expenses along with your debts (credit cards, mortgages, car loans, school loans, etc.) and any fixed or foreseeable expenses. Everyone's situation is different and there is no right way to organize your finances, but without some planning and organization, an unexpected expense can wreak havoc on a household that is merely gliding from paycheck to paycheck.

2. Track Your Spending: Keep note of what you're currently spending your money on. A $10 expense once a week may not seem very noticeable, but when you're spending over $500 a year, then you may determine that that money is better being saved or paying off debt.

3. Stop Unnecessary Spending: Cut out frivolous spending where you can. If it isn't essential, chances are you don't need to have it. By working off a budget and tracking your expenses, you'll see how much you're paying for non-essential expenses, such as subscription services, ordering takeout, or entertainment purchases.

4. Live Frugally: Scale back on your flexible essential expenses and find ways to stretch how far your money goes. Here are some ideas: switch to a cheaper cell phone plan, downgrade your internet service, stop eating out and cook at home, choose generic over name brands, turn off lights and other electronics, and cancel subscription services you don't use often.

5. Set an Achievable Goal: Setting individual goals can help motivate you to save. Some different types of goals are creating a budget, paying off debt, creating an emergency fund, saving for retirement or for a short-term goal, and building good credit. Defining and mapping out ways to achieve your goals makes reaching them easier.

6. Review Your Budget: Track your current expenses to get a clear view of the impact of inflation on your wallet. Some of the best apps designed to track your spending will also offer budgeting tools for free.

Money can't buy happiness—although it is cliché, it remains true. Being rich will not necessarily make you happier. But It will increase your standard of living and evaluation of life. What can help make an individual happy is making good financial decisions.

Your financial situation and mental health go hand-in-hand. If you are able to keep yourself from needlessly facing major financial issues, you are less likely to face mental health issues. I work with women and families every day to map out a new financial future for themselves and their families. Financial wellness is achievable. It does take intentional actions, but you can rewrite your financial path.

Now let's look at what has been holding us back as women in a man's world!

As women we have come a long way, but we can do better. A recent study, which included surveys of nearly 1,700 married couples, including heterosexual and same-sex couples, showed that Millennial women are more likely to leave investment decisions to their husbands than any other age group. I find this extremely concerning because women are living longer than men. The average life expectancy for a woman is at least five years more than a man's, not to mention divorce rates have doubled since the '90s, maybe even tripled following the pandemic. Given these two factors alone, 8 out of 10 women will end up alone and solely responsible for their families and their own financial well-being. Therefore, a lack of knowledge of your financial situation or awareness can be catastrophic.

I have sat across the table from many women who are lost, overwhelmed, and stuck rebuilding. Nearly 60% of widows and divorcees said they wish they had been more involved in the financial planning decisions, with 56% of women discovering hidden debt, inadequate savings, or overly conservative or aggressive investments that affected their lifestyle and retirement goals.

It's not as if we aren't contributing funds or touching money at all. In fact, most of us are completely comfortable and savvy in handling the bulk of the household's day-to-day finances and contributing half or more to the budget. But when it comes to planning for retirement or investment, there is a disconnect. I am not saying don't plan with your significant other. You both should be working toward a common goal. However, trusting and being led blindly into your future financial wellness with no checks and balances can lead to failure.

Gender roles are certainly hard to shake, with men traditionally handling the long-term financial planning decisions instead of their wives. Men also tend to make more money than women, but even though they were the breadwinners, that reality has changed. So, why are female breadwinners or equal breadwinners still leaving financial decisions to their husbands? What I have found is that it is more about a lack of confidence.

We need to change our money mindset and approach, let go of our old negative ideals, and develop a more positive relationship with money. No one, male or female, needs to be an expert to handle retirement and investment decisions. You just need to ask the right questions, gain some basic financial literacy, engage in your finances, and take an active role.

Aside from making the decision to take an active role in your financial wellness, you need to set goals and make a plan of action to follow. Even though we may still live in a man-driven world, that does not mean we can't as women rise above social norms. After making the decision to take an active role in building your legacy, you need to understand your FIN (Financial Independence Number). I am sure you are wondering what I am talking about. Your FIN is the amount you will need to retire, or become independent from your current income, in a nutshell. Everyone's FIN is different based on their needs, wants, and obligations. The rule of thumb is: Financial

independence is when you save roughly 25 times your annual spending. At this point, your finances are independent of your paycheck. Once you understand where you need to be, then we can decide where you want to be in the future.

While deciding to take control of your financial world can seem overwhelming, there are some basic steps we can take. Look at manageable things in our lives. What are some easy steps you could take to get started and not be overwhelmed during the process? Feeling in control of and confident about your financial situation will help you achieve that money mindset.

Spend Intentionally: If you don't need it, consider holding off on any new purchases until you can get the best deal. Wait until prices settle down to make big-ticket purchases, such as a new car or home improvement materials.

Be Flexible: Consider substituting used goods you can buy through online platforms or at thrift stores for non-food items like clothing, furniture, housewares, etc. Try eating at home instead of eating out. If you do eat out, drink water instead of colas, tea, or alcohol to save.

Change Your Habits: Consolidate errands and use public transportation, when possible, to use less gas. Use fans and open windows instead of turning on the air conditioning when it's hot and use blankets or layers to keep warm when it's cold before turning on the heat. To save on water, take shorter showers, and run full loads of laundry and dishes.

Through a change in money mindset, taking an active role in your financial future, planning, taking actionable steps, securing wealth, encouraging financial literacy at home, and communication, you are well on your way to building a legacy. We don't plan to fail but we do often fail to plan. Through faith in yourself, focus on your mission and intentional actions and you will see growth. If you have questions, concerns, or need some guidance, please reach out and mention this book/chapter to get a complementary Financial Needs Assessment to get you on your path to wellness!

I have had to rebuild several times in life. That is why I help families go from surviving to thriving and building generational wealth.

Sylvia Becker-Hill

Founder of Becker-Hill Inc.

https://www.linkedin.com/in/sylviabeckerhill/
https://www.facebook.com/sylvia.beckerhill/
https://www.instagram.com/sylviabeckerhill/
www.becker-hill.comwww.sylviabecker-hill.com

Sylvia Becker-Hill is a true Renaissance woman, a multiple-published bestselling author, and a seasoned edutainer who has empowered thousands of corporate executives, women leaders, and entrepreneurs around the world since 1997. In 2002, she became the first German coach to earn the coveted title of Professional Certified Coach from the International Coach Federation, establishing herself as a pioneer in the coaching world. Her impressive educational background boasts two university degrees, while her portfolio showcases over 30 certifications in various change modalities, including her accreditation as one of the world's first 10 Certified Master Neuroplasticians in 2023. Sylvia's mission is to empower you with all the knowledge, tools, and lasting transformation you need to "FLIP" everything that bothers, hurts, or blocks you from living your desires and dreams into unquestionable Freedom, unconditional Love, envisioned Identity, and impactful Power. Are you ready to discover the joy of feeling unabashedly alive and powerful?

THE PRICE OF SHAME: HOW YOUR BODY IMAGE IMPACTS YOUR FINANCIAL SUCCESS

By Sylvia Becker-Hill

"Unless we change course, humanity will set foot on Mars before achieving global pay equity for women of all races. This is utterly unacceptable!"
—Sylvia Becker-Hill

The Challenge: Bridging the Gender Wealth Gap

Despite women outnumbering men in colleges across many developed countries and legal mandates for equal compensation, the persistent gender wealth gap remains a troubling reality. Depending on factors like skin color, age, and geographic location, women continue to earn 55% to 10% less per dollar per hour than their male counterparts.

But why does this gap persist?

The answer is multifaceted and varies from one country to another. In this chapter, I delve into a unique perspective born from my own extensive research—a viewpoint rarely explored elsewhere: the image of our female body in our own perception and that of society throughout history!

We can all acknowledge the gravity of the gender pay and wealth gaps:

- Senior women are more likely to live below the poverty line than men.
- Fewer women ascend to top leadership positions across all sectors.
- Societies with entrenched gender disparities often see bullies thrive and male leaders instigate conflicts.
- Healthcare systems prioritize research on men's health, neglecting the specific needs of women.
- Political landscapes suffer from a shortage of female representation, hindering progress on critical issues like climate change.

Is this a grim portrayal? Undoubtedly.

One too big to be related to women's income? Absolutely not.

Global statistics from reputable organizations like the World Health Organization and the United Nations reveal a compelling truth: When women and girls flourish—safely, healthily, educationally, and financially—entire societies thrive harmoniously. The gender pay and wealth gaps serve as barometers of humanity's progress on a grand scale.

Your earnings as a woman compared to a man's under identical circumstances serve as a Key Performance Indicator (KPI) for our collective evolution toward a peaceful, equitable world. KPIs are vital, quantifiable measures of progress toward a desired outcome.

Why do I present such a vast context? Because I want you to understand that your financial challenges and aspirations are not merely personal burdens—they are significant. You matter, and so does the collective journey we are on. Our pursuit of fulfillment and happiness intertwines with the betterment of the world and the legacy we leave for future generations.

The encouraging news amidst these challenges is that progress is underway, albeit gradual. In the pages ahead, I will outline how you can accelerate this progress through personal transformation.

The perspective I offer for overcoming your financial obstacles is unique and may challenge your preconceptions. I urge you to approach this chapter with an open mind, donning your researcher's hat. Engage not only intellectually but also "chew" on the content I present, so that your body shows you where it resonates.

The Pink Money Elephant in the Room

"As long as the women's empowerment industry ignores the 'money elephant' in the room, we'll keep missing the true cause of women's financial stagnation!"
—Sylvia Becker-Hill

In my view, there's a glaring blind spot in the women's empowerment industry: While well-intentioned financial advisors provide valuable guidance on banking products, investing, saving, and retirement planning, much of this information is readily available for free. Yet, despite the accessibility of resources through books, YouTube, and workshops, many women fail to take action.

Countless coaches focus on addressing women's money mindset, helping them overcome inherited beliefs and mental blocks around finances. This work is undeniably beneficial, but it comes at a cost. Coaching is often expensive, leaving only a select few able to afford it.

Moreover, even profound shifts in mindset don't always translate into tangible changes in financial behavior.

I found myself on both sides of this equation: investing in expensive coaching and materials to reshape my money mindset, while also providing similar services to empower other women. While some experienced significant financial breakthroughs, others continued to struggle. It became evident to me that there was a recurring blind spot within myself, within our society, and within the women's empowerment industry.

One evening, in the midst of frustration and worry about my own financial stability, I turned to my subconscious for answers. I posed a question laying in bed, seeking insight beyond my rational mind. The next morning, I awoke to a clear message resonating in my mind:

"As long as women don't start talking about money as casually and gracefully with each other as they do about their hair and clothes, the patriarchy will always win."

This revelation hit me like a thunderbolt. It revealed a fundamental truth: **Women don't openly discuss money, not even with their closest friends.**

Now, ponder these questions slowly:

- How do you negotiate a higher salary if discussions about money are taboo?
- If you're self-employed, how do you demand better fees or prices without openly discussing money?
- How do you secure better deals with suppliers or negotiate favorable mortgages if money remains a forbidden topic?
- How can you prevent the financial conflicts that often lead to divorce if discussing money with your spouse triggers drama?

- How do you instill financial literacy in your children if conversations about money are off-limits?

Take a deep breath and reflect on two critical questions:

How would your life change if you could freely discuss money with anyone?

How would the world transform if all women could openly discuss money without hesitation?

Our minds and voices are fully capable; we converse daily on a multitude of topics. Yet, when it comes to money, a curious silence ensues. Why the reluctance?

After wrestling with my own doubts for several days, I decided to heed the advice of my muse and embark on an experiment. I created a Facebook group called "Money Talks" and launched a year-long initiative: bi-weekly live discussions on Zoom dedicated solely to money matters. The insights gained from this endeavor form the basis of this chapter, aiming to unravel the following:

What silences us when it comes to money?

How can we shatter this "glass ceiling of silence" to reclaim our financial power?

Shifting Paradigms:
The Changing Perception of Women's Bodies in Society

*"Since the end of matriarchies, our bodies have
stopped being our own."*
—Sylvia Becker-Hill

I invite you to follow along with the exploration of the evolution of society's perception of women's bodies. As a scholar of gender studies, with roots in pioneering research in Germany during the late '90s, and having delved into matriarchal cultures for my master's thesis, I offer a bold historical overview—one that may initially seem foreign, even unsettling, but ultimately resolves into a beautiful and powerful narrative.

 ## Women's Societal Body Image 1:
Honoring Its Fertility, Nurturance, and Life-Giving Essence

Our journey commences approximately 29,000 to 7,000 years ago, a period marked by the awe-inspiring artifacts known as "Venus" or "Goddess Figurines" by archaeologists. While their precise significance remains subject to debate, their widespread presence across diverse geographies and societies offers compelling insights:

The creation of images, art, or tools depicting women signifies a form of human expression that reflects societal values and priorities.

Envision these simplified graphics inspired by ancient artifacts. Can you sense the reverence, the adoration, the inherent beauty attributed to women's bodies by both the artisans and their respective societies? The ample breasts and hips symbolize the importance of fat reserves for surviving harsh conditions and nurturing offspring. Sagging breasts denote veneration for elderly women and their maternal contributions to their tribes.

Women were revered as sacred embodiments of the divine Mother Goddess—symbols of fertility, abundance, and the nurturing essence of Mother Nature. They held a higher status than men, who were perceived merely as mortal beings.

Take a deep breath and gaze lovingly upon your own body. Does your perception shift knowing the profound reverence with which women's bodies were once regarded?

2 Women's Societal Body Image 2: Reduced to Instruments of Reproduction in Times of Conflict

Tragically, the egalitarian matriarchal societies that thrived for nearly 50,000 years faced upheaval as climate crises spurred migrations and conflicts over scarce resources. The advent of metalwork and weapon crafting around 7,000 years ago ushered in an era of brutal warfare, marking a stark departure from earlier times when archaeologists found no evidence of violent deaths in graves. The era of global peace among small tribes, each comprising around 120 members at most, came to an end as communities grew, requiring more land and resources.

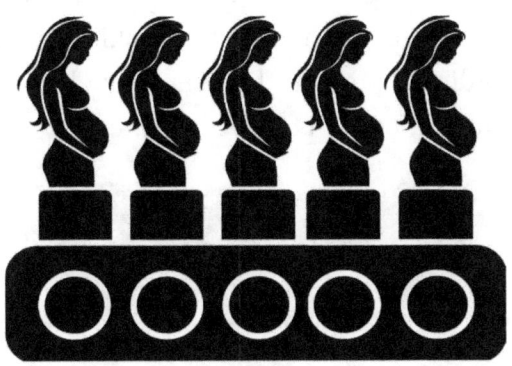

Organized religion, influenced by patriarchal values, supplanted the nurturing mother goddess with a stern father deity. Consequently, women's status plummeted, relegating them beneath men in the societal hierarchy. No longer revered as embodiments of the Divine Goddess, women became mere vessels, their bodies commodified and controlled by landowners, kings, and military leaders. Perceived as "breeding machines," women were tasked with bearing the next generation of soldiers and laborers, replenishing populations decimated by violent conflicts and wars.

3 Women's Societal Body Image 3: The Estrangement from Nature and the Stigmatization of Women's Bodies

Regrettably, humanity's once harmonious relationship with the divine and the natural world devolved into disconnection and fear. No longer viewed as a direct, intimate connection, the perception of nature shifted, becoming tinged with apprehension and the need for control.

This psychological and cultural shift created a chasm between individuals and higher powers, often mediated by those in positions of authority—kings, priests, shamans, and, later, academics and scientists. Once revered as nurturing and supportive, nature came to be seen as something to be feared, tamed, and conquered following climatic upheavals like the Ice Age. Women, whose bodies aligned with the lunar cycles and possessed the ability to bear children, became symbols of nature's unpredictable power. Their monthly bleeding and the act of childbirth were irrationally perceived as threats.

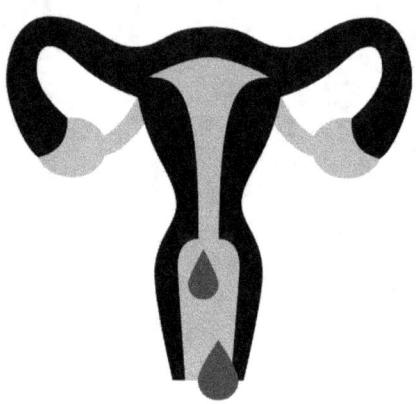

These irrational fears manifested in various forms within society—disgust at menstrual bleeding, fear of women's reproductive capabilities, and even envy of their life-giving abilities. The infamous witch hunts spanning 300 years from 1450 to 1750, resulting in the deaths of approximately 50,000 women (with unrecorded lynchings estimated to be in the multiple six figures!), epitomized society's irrational and hostile attitudes toward women's bodies.

Unfortunately, remnants of this negative perception persist, perpetuated by fundamentalist groups harboring deep-seated insecurities and fears, which they unreflectively project onto women's bodies.

4 Women's Societal Body Image 4: Women as Commodities: Bartering for Money and Status

Not too long ago—sadly, in some countries still—daughters were treated as commodities, sold by their fathers to the highest bidders. The price was often determined by notions of "purity of mind" and "intact sexual virginity." This normalized form of sex trafficking persisted for centuries across many societies, with the concept of "love matches" and "marriages by choice" emerging relatively recently. Echoes of this tradition linger in certain societal circles, where extremely young and conventionally beautiful women are paraded as "trophy wives" alongside older, affluent men. In such contexts, a woman's body is viewed as a means to procure money and status for her husband.

5 Women's Societal Body Image 5: Objects of Male Pleasure and Stress Relief

In the wake of movements like #MeToo and the heightened public awareness surrounding sexism, misogyny, and violence against women and girls, it's challenging for young women today to comprehend what was once considered normal in patriarchal societies.

For centuries, women's bodies were regarded as acceptable tools for the pleasure and stress relief of men. The notion that women own their bodies, can experience orgasms, possess a highly sensitive organ—the clitoris—designed for their pleasure, and are free to pursue pleasure on their own terms or with consenting partners are all relatively recent discoveries, emerging in the past 70 years.

6 Women's Societal Body Image 6: Capitalizing on Objectification: The Marketplace of Female Consumption

Since the 1970s, when women in most countries worldwide gained the right to earn and control their own money, open bank accounts, start businesses, and pursue corporate careers, the capitalist marketplace has recognized women's bodies as a lucrative avenue for driving consumption.

Industries spanning from fashion and beauty to household goods and automobiles have capitalized on women's bodies to sell products. The fashion and beauty sectors, in particular, have perpetuated doctrines of beauty and perfectionism, which not only objectify women's bodies but also serve to oppress and consume women's attention, time, and financial resources.

7 Women's Societal Body Image 7: Political Pawn: Women's Bodies in Power Struggles

In recent years, we have witnessed a troubling political backlash against the feminist movement and its advocacy for equality, diversity, and inclusion in women's rights, safety, and access to resources. Nowhere is this more evident than in debates over reproductive rights, where women's bodies have become political bargaining chips in power struggles.

But what does this history of societal perceptions of women's bodies have to do with our inability as women to openly discuss money and your own aspirations for financial stability and freedom? Everything.

Thanks to the pioneering work of figures like C.G. Jung, we now understand that our immensely powerful **subconscious minds** connect us to the **collective subconsciousness of all women—**past and present. **Our collective history resides within us, emotionally and energetically stored in our subconscious minds.**

As you reflect on the history of society's perception and treatment of women's bodies, I urge you to delve deeper than mere words and facts.

What emotions do you feel after reading my bold historic summary?

What relationship have we, as women, developed with our bodies as a result of this collective history?

What mindset and attitude have we, as a gender, adopted toward our bodies?

Mirror Mirror on the Wall

"How we treat our body is how we treat our money."
—Sylvia Becker-Hill

It's fascinating to uncover these profound connections in our consciousness, where one relationship mirrors the structure of another. I believe it stems from our brain's innate design principle, which seeks to conserve energy by simplifying its operations. Just as we create templates in design software, our brains establish mirroring operating systems in our daily lives, maintaining consistent forms, structures, and processes in order to save energy!

When I speak with women about their relationships with their bodies, it becomes painfully clear **that our collective perception is deeply ingrained with outdated cultural conditioning.** Despite our conscious beliefs, women often harbor subconscious notions that our bodies are "bad," "dirty," "dangerous," "sinful," "in need of fixing," "not beautiful enough," and ultimately "owned by men."

In the margins of this book or, ideally, in a dedicated journal, I invite you to complete the following sentence as a writing prompt: **"Money is ..."** Repeat this exercise at least 50 times, allowing your thoughts to flow freely and writing swiftly by hand, without overthinking it. Then, take a moment to review what you've written.

How many parallels can you observe and feel between your relationship with money and your relationship with your body?

The Emotion that Keeps Women Mute About Money

"The loss of ownership over our own bodies is equivalent to the loss of sovereignty over ourselves. It triggers the belief that 'There must be something wrong with me.'
The emotional reaction to that loss is SHAME, which is deeply ingrained in our collective subconsciousness as women."
—Sylvia Becker-Hill

Beneath all our beliefs about our bodies and money lies a potent emotion: shame.

In literature, we often encounter the dichotomy of love and fear. However, in my experience, the opposite of love isn't fear, but shame. Love fosters connection, peace, fulfillment, and growth, while shame breeds separation, turmoil, inadequacy, and contraction. It compels us to hide, to shrink into ourselves, and to devise avoidance strategies.

Above all, **shame silences us—it's the ultimate mute maker.**

This insidious emotion, once planted by oppressors, thrives within us, robbing us of our voices and rendering us powerless. Its strength lies in our inability to name it, keeping us trapped in its suffocating grip and in place, rendering us powerless.

That's why **the first step toward empowerment and breaking the silence is acknowledgment: "I feel shame."** Whether it's confronting our naked reflection in the mirror or assessing our financial situation, we must confront our shame head-on. So, pause for a moment and delve beneath the surface of your financial reality. What do you truly feel?

Do you recall the Brothers Grimm fairy tale of Rumpelstiltskin? In it, a farmer's daughter, gifted with the ability to spin straw into gold, finds herself ensnared in a pact with a magic gnome. When the time comes to repay her debt with her firstborn child, she's thrust into desperation. However, by uncovering the gnome's secret name and calling it out loud—Rumpelstiltskin!—she shatters his power and secures her child's safety and her freedom to live happily ever after.

I love this fairytale, not only because I'm German and grew up with it, but rather because it shows so clearly **the power we have over things when we address them head-on!**

Calling things out gives us power over them! When you can feel and fully own the shame about your body and your money and admit it, you break its crippling muting spell on you!

Confidence is the Best Makeup

"As soon a woman can look lovingly at her body without shame, she finds her voice of confidence to talk about money and will ask for more."
—Sylvia Becker-Hill

Becoming a confident, sensually liberated woman begins with letting go of shame about your body and embracing it as the miracle it truly is. When you fall utterly in love with your body, your confidence will soar, and your sense of enoughness will stabilize. A woman who feels good in her body naturally becomes a powerful negotiator, especially when it comes to money.

Let me share a true story from my own life to give you a taste of what this confidence and sensuality might look like:

I had just secured a top executive in the automotive supplier industry as my client, agreeing to my largest coaching package yet—$16,000. Feeling triumphant, I decided to treat myself to a luxurious purchase: a gorgeous white quilted designer coat with a fur-trimmed hood. As I drove home, clad only in my old boots and the new coat, I felt like a modern-day Lara Croft—beautiful, powerful, and aroused.

Upon arriving home, I wasted no time. I pulled my husband from his home office, wordlessly leading him to our bedroom. With him lying in bed, his eyes wide with surprise and delight, I opened my coat to reveal my naked body underneath.

"Honey," I whispered, "I just sold $16,000 worth of coaching. I feel amazing and want to celebrate with you."

The rest I leave to your imagination… :-)

Becoming this kind of confident, sensual woman requires **a journey of self-discovery and self-love**. It involves embracing your body, celebrating your sensuality, and cultivating an unshakeable sense of confidence in yourself and your worth. It's about reclaiming your power and expressing yourself authentically in every aspect of your life.

To empower you with a practical tool, from the years of my own journey I created the **"Money-Body-Love Manifesto"** outlined below, plus this list of **"Seven Wealth Empowering Actions:"**

1. **Leave Shame Behind:** Embrace your body as the miraculous vessel it is. Release shame about your body and its relationship with money.

2. **Forgive Yourself:** Feel compassion for past mistakes you might have made regarding money. You didn't know what you didn't know. Blaming yourself would keep you stuck in shame. Forgiveness is the key that breaks the shackle.

3. **Share This Book:** Share this book with your girlfriends. Spark conversations and support one another on your journey to financial and personal empowerment.

4. **Start a Book Club:** Begin a book club to discuss each chapter. Dive deep into the content, share insights, and learn from one another's perspectives.

5. **Find an Accountability Buddy:** Partner with a girlfriend as your accountability buddy and intentionally talk about money when you see each other. Encourage each other, celebrate wins, and navigate challenges together.

6. **Initiate a Money Talks Group:** Launch your own Money Talks Group, either online or in person. Create a safe, confidential space where you and your girlfriends can openly discuss money—from making and saving it to managing and investing it.

7. **Surround Yourself with Mentors:** Mentors are women or men who are at the place you want to get to. Follow them and create relationships with them, allowing yourself to be inspired and empowered by their examples.

By embracing these principles and actions, you'll not only transform your own life but also contribute to a **global movement of Money Talkers**. Together, we will heal the collective subconscious of women—one Money Talk at a time. If you decide to start a Money Talks Group, don't hesitate to reach out to me. I may even join a meeting to empower your group further!

Your Money-Body-Love Manifesto^{TM}

"When a woman speaks her money-body-love manifesto for 90 days deeply into her own eyes while using her breath to create somatic alignment within her body, her finances will change for the better."
—Sylvia Becker-Hill

Please stand in front of a mirror and look deeply into your left eye. Read the following words into it loud and confidently while exuding love for your body. Breathe deeply between each sentence. Use interoception to sense inside your body any friction or tension indicating resistance against a statement. See if you can simply let go of the resistance. If not, use your breath, allowing love to flood the area of your body where you sense misalignment, until all tension gently evaporates.

Maybe a slightly different wording (or use your mother language if different from English) is more powerful for you! Feel free to rephrase the manifesto while keeping the essence of the meaning intact until the words feel right in your body. Words are powerful! **They are like magic spells that create reality when combined with intentionality and in alignment with your body's well-being.**

"I am a spiritual being inhabiting a human body.
With each breath, I honor the divine essence within me."

"My body is beautiful, regardless of its appearance.
I celebrate its unique characteristics and embrace every curve and contour."

"I love and cherish my body, recognizing its innate worth and value.

I am the sole owner of my body, and I confidently assert
my rights over it."

"I am safe and free to love, care for, and speak openly about my body.
I honor its needs and nurture it with kindness and compassion."

"I am empowered to discuss money openly and freely
with anyone I choose.
I release any fears or inhibitions surrounding financial conversations."

"I choose to love and appreciate money, independent of familial or
cultural beliefs.
I welcome abundance into my life with open arms."

"I take joy in negotiating, saving, investing,
and managing my finances.
I am confident in my ability to handle money wisely
and responsibly."

"Every day, I expand my knowledge and understanding of my
body and finances.
I am committed to lifelong learning and growth in these areas."

"I embrace my role as an unapologetic woman,
prioritizing the health of my body and the growth of my wealth."

"I celebrate my journey with gratitude and determination.
Failing forward makes my success inevitable."

If you want a beautifully designed poster of The Money-Body-Love Manifesto to print and frame, you can download it here:

A Letter from Sylvia to You

Dear Reader,

I wrote this chapter with the intention to empower you to fall in love with your beautiful miraculous body AND with the freedom and impact-power that money as a resource can provide you.

Did I succeed?

Did you experience some flashes of insights that jolted not only your brain but also your body?

Can you see how your treatment of your body and your treatment of money have patterns that mirror each other?

Did you receive enough ideas to start changing both relationships?

Reading without implementation is just fleeting entertainment.

Will you start a circle with friends, meeting over lunch or dinner at minimum once a month, and learn to simply openly talk about your finances, share your worries and your dreams, talking numbers?

Or a monthly book club to learn together from money-focused books starting with this one, The Female Money Playbook?

Or start a savings club for accountability?

Or an investment club for leveraging combined assets?

Will you learn about your and your spouse's money personality and train yourself and invite him to do the same to have unemotional, drama-free (!), simple conversations about your finances to divorce-proof your marriage?

*I know I ask for a lot of impact from just a chapter... yet **I do care about you.***

*I know that every one of us women liberating herself and **talking freely about money from within a body we love, free from shame, is liberating our collective subconsciousness as women.***

We are in this together, Dear Star-Sister!

So please do reach out and tell me what you took from this chapter and what your questions are!

You can reach me at sylvia@becker-hill.com. Write "Female Money Playbook" in the subject line and I'll know you read my chapter. You never know, maybe I'll join one of your groups as a speaker for a Q&A or come to your company as a keynote speaker...if we run into each other at a women's empowerment conference, please introduce yourself as one of my readers.

I can't wait to meet you!

xoxo,
Sylvia

Niurka Coteron

Unstoppable Being LLC & Insightful CFO, LLC
Business Growth and Wealth Strategist

www.linkedin.com/in/niurka-coteron-emba-cfo-cfe-cpa-a239025/
https://www.facebook.com/niurka.coteron
https://www.instagram.com/niurkacoteron/
www.insightfulcfo.com
www.unstoppablebeing.com

Niurka Coteron is a distinguished business and growth strategist, transformation catalyst, and seasoned business mentor with over 35 years of notable career achievements. Excelling in executive leadership and global industry consulting across public, private, and non-profit sectors, she's left an enduring impact. Author of "Begin From Within," available on Amazon, Niurka shines as a luminary in her field. Her international speaking engagements and collaboration with other women captivates audiences with profound insights. She is recognized with esteemed accolades and showcases extensive business knowledge and dedication to empowering women to become millionaires. As Founder and CEO of Insightful CFO, LLC, Niurka expertly leads professional accounting and management consulting. Her firm helps business entrepreneurs make informed decisions and manage their financial operation effectively by identifying business gaps, optimizing operational excellence and profitability. Additionally, as the visionary behind Unstoppable Being, LLC, Niurka empowers women through coaching, workshops, and digital courses, fostering confidence, leadership, and intentional life design to make millions. Her academic achievements include an Executive Master of Business Administration from Strayer University and Jack Welch Management Institute and two Bachelor of Science in Accounting and Finance from Rutgers University. She acquired a certificate in Women's Entrepreneurship from Cornell University. She holds various certifications in the financial field.

THE JOURNEY OF MONEY: A REFUGEE'S TALE

By Niurka Coteron

Our lives will be changed in the next five years by the people we meet and the books we read. Make It – Keep It – Grow It has been my motto for money and my life mission while supporting women entrepreneurs in doing the same.

When I first set foot on American soil, I was a teenager with nothing but hope and a burning desire to succeed. My family had fled Cuba, leaving everything we knew in search of a better life. Unfortunately, the Cuban government left my mother behind, breaking the family unit. But as we arrived in New Jersey, the harsh reality of our situation set in. We were refugees, starting over with no mother, no money, no connections, and no clear path forward.

In Cuba, money had been a distant concept. We survived by bartering and with the little money my father could earn. But here, in the bustling streets of New Jersey, money was the lifeblood of existence. Without it, survival seemed impossible. As a teenager, I quickly grasped the value of every dollar and cent as I entered the world with a powerful thrust.

Growing up, I often had to rely on school lunches because we had no money for anything else. My friends, who were also refugees, and I longed for the occasional treat from the corner hot dog truck. We decided to go together one day, but I needed $2 to join them. When I asked my father for the money, he agreed to give it to me. However, the next morning, I discovered that my father had gone to work without leaving the $2. Whether it was an oversight or simply that he forgot, I was consumed with anger and shame. I couldn't bear the thought of facing my friends and admitting that I was too poor to join them. Overwhelmed by my feelings, I chose not to go to school that day, hoping to hide my embarrassment and the harsh reality of my family's financial struggles.

With the decision to avoid school that day, I also made other subconscious decisions that would shape my life forever. I was operating on decisions hidden from my view.

The first decision was that I would make so much money that I would never have to rely on anyone. This decision led to a relentless drive for financial independence, pushing me to excel academically and professionally. I pursued every opportunity with an enthusiasm that set me apart from my peers. The rewards were significant: a successful career, financial stability, and a sense of personal achievement that bolstered my confidence and self-worth.

The second decision, however, was that men are unreliable, and I couldn't count on them. This belief influenced my relationships profoundly. I approached interactions with men with skepticism and guardedness, often building emotional walls that were hard to breach. This decision led to missed opportunities for meaningful connections and fostered a sense of isolation. Trust issues became a recurring theme in my personal life, causing strain in friendships and romantic relationships. It wasn't until much later in adulthood that I began to recognize these patterns and understand that they were rooted in that pivotal day's subconscious choices. Recognizing these decisions allowed me to start healing and redefining my perceptions, but the journey was challenging and required substantial self-reflection and effort to overcome the ingrained mistrust.

As time passed, based on one of those two decisions, my life became about learning about money—how to make, keep, and grow it.

My first job was at a local grocery store. I remember the interview vividly, my palms sweating and my heart racing as I tried to explain with my limited English why, at 14 years old, I wanted to work. The manager, a kind-hearted pregnant woman named Mrs. Alonso, saw something in me and gave me a chance. I started as a bagger, earning minimum wage at $3.10 per hour. It wasn't much, but it was a start. Ms. Alonso was the daughter of the store owner.

Every day after school, I rushed to the store. I bagged groceries, stocked shelves, and cleaned floors until about 9 pm, and for half a day on Saturdays. The work was grueling, but it taught me discipline and the importance of hard work. Then, an opportunity opened, and I became a cashier.

I learned to budget my earnings, saving every penny I could. I resisted the temptation to spend on things my peers enjoyed—movies, fast food, new clothes. Instead, I focused on essentials: contributing to the rent, buying groceries, and saving for the future.

My father found work, too, but it was never enough. We struggled to make ends meet, often walking instead of taking the bus to save money. Despite the hardships, we remained hopeful. We were determined to build a new life, which meant understanding and mastering the concept of money.

I felt fortunate to have found a job and enjoyed lunch with my school friends some days. It was a slight sense of normalcy in my upside-down world.

However, my luck did not last long. A few months into my new job, I began to feel increasingly uncomfortable due to the inappropriate behavior of the manager's husband. He often lingered around the cash register, waiting until I was alone. The space behind the counter was very narrow, and he would use this to his advantage, pressing up against me as he pretended to reach for something or squeeze past me unnecessarily. His behavior was invasive and persistent, making it clear that it wasn't accidental.

Every time I saw him approach, a knot of anxiety would form in my stomach. I would try to position myself in a way that minimized contact, but it was impossible to avoid him entirely in such a confined space. The feeling of his presence behind me, his breath too close for comfort, made my skin crawl. I felt trapped and powerless, unable to speak out for fear of losing the job I was so grateful to have.

The dread I felt each day began to overshadow the joy I had initially experienced from having a job. What was once a place where I felt proud and independent had become a source of stress and fear. The tension and discomfort became unbearable, and I realized I couldn't continue working in such an environment. Despite needing the income, I had to prioritize my safety and well-being.

Finally, I made the difficult decision to quit. It was a painful choice, but I knew it was necessary. The experience left me shaken, but it also made me more determined to find a place to work without fear and with the respect I deserved.

After quitting my job as a cashier, I decided to take a bold step and become an entrepreneur. My first business idea was simple but effective: I contacted each building owner in my neighborhood to see if they wanted me to clean their building stairs. Armed with determination and a willingness to work hard, I knocked on doors and pitched my services.

To my surprise, the response was overwhelmingly positive. Many building owners were eager to hire someone reliable to clean their staircases. I quickly lined up several clients and began working diligently. Suddenly, I was making more per hour than I ever did working as a cashier. The freedom of being my own boss and the satisfaction of seeing my hard work pay off were incredibly empowering.

My small business steadily grew as word spread about my quality service and dedication. I took pride in every job I completed, and the positive feedback from my clients fueled my ambition. What started as a modest cleaning service soon expanded, and I began to think about other opportunities to grow and diversify my business.

Looking back, quitting my job as a cashier was a turning point. It was a difficult and frightening decision, but it led me to discover my entrepreneurial spirit and carve out a path for myself that was both rewarding and fulfilling.

In school, I took every opportunity to learn about finance. I attended workshops, read books, and sought advice from teachers. One day, a teacher named Mr. Diaz introduced me to investing. He explained how money could grow over time if wisely invested. Intrigued, I started researching. I opened a small savings account and deposited some of my monthly earnings. The interest was minimal, but it was a start. I started a holiday club to help me save for holiday shopping. It allowed me to make weekly deposits until it was distributed right before the holiday season, making my shopping more pleasant.

Years passed, and I graduated high school. I continued working part-time while studying business, accounting, and finance at the university. The lessons I learned were invaluable. I began to understand the stock market, the importance of credit, and how to manage debt. Slowly but surely, I built a small but growing investment portfolio, and by the age of 20, I had purchased my first real estate investment income-producing property using debt from a bank.

However, despite my best efforts, my money was not growing fast enough. Even with all the education, I didn't know how much money I would need to earn and save to stop working eventually with family, a mortgage, and many more responsibilities. As a single mother with three children, the pressure was immense. Balancing the demands of work and raising my kids meant there was little room for error, and every financial decision carried significant weight. I felt an urgent need to break away from the path that society had laid out: get a job, pay bills, save, and invest. No matter how much money I made, it was never enough.

To address this, I realized I needed a more strategic approach. First, I sought financial advice to create a comprehensive plan tailored to my needs and goals. These included setting clear, achievable financial milestones and understanding the power of compound interest. I diversified my investments to balance risk and reward, explored additional passive income streams such as dividend-paying stocks, and adopted a more frugal lifestyle to maximize savings, making all these tasks very automatic, reducing my efforts and energy.

Additionally, I focused on improving my financial literacy, staying informed about market trends, and reassessing my financial plan regularly to ensure it aligned with my changing circumstances. Juggling work and raising three kids taught me the value of time management and prioritization, which I also applied to my financial strategy. By taking these proactive steps, I aimed to build a more secure financial future for my family and achieve true financial independence, ensuring that my children would have the opportunities they deserved without the constant stress of financial instability.

In addition to my financial strategy, I recognized the importance of securing life insurance to safeguard my family's future and provide peace of mind. As a single mother with three children, ensuring they would be financially protected if something happened to me was crucial. I explored various life insurance options, ultimately selecting policies that offered substantial coverage at affordable premiums. This way, I could guarantee that my children would have the financial resources to cover living expenses, education costs, and other essential needs, even in my absence. Additionally, I chose life insurance instruments that would benefit me later in life, offering a source of funds for retirement or emergencies. By incorporating life insurance into my financial plan, I gained a mindset of freedom, knowing that my loved ones would be supported and secure and have a financial safety net in my later years, allowing me to focus on building a stable future without constant worry, no matter what uncertainties life might bring.

Then, I put all my efforts into making enough money to cover everything, strategically delegating tasks to maximize efficiency and productivity. By outsourcing specific responsibilities and seeking help where needed, I could focus on high-impact activities that significantly boosted my income. This approach allowed me to balance my time between work, family, and personal development more effectively. Delegating not only eased my workload but also enabled me to leverage the skills and expertise of others, propelling me toward my financial goals at a much faster pace. This shift in strategy resulted in a quantum leap in my life, transforming my financial stability and overall well-being.

Today, I help women to navigate the complex world of money. I often remember my teenage years, our struggles, and the determination that drove us. Once an elusive and daunting concept, money has become a tool I use to build a better life for myself and others. The journey was never easy, but it taught me resilience, discipline, and the actual value of money. It also gave me freedom of choice.

Often, my clients think they want more money, and I usually tell them it's not more money they want; what they want is what money can get them. It's vital to understand that pursuing more money isn't the ultimate goal, and nobody earns their way to freedom by earning or saving money. Yes, we have to save money and then convert it into assets. The goal is to have assets because assets give you these four freedoms integral to a truly fulfilling life.

Time Freedom: Yes, money can buy you back more time. Time is the only resource we can't get more of. You're sacrificing your most valuable asset when trading 50 to 60 hours a week for money just to survive. Imagine being able to design your days, follow your passions, and be present for life's most important moments. Imagine also being able to say yes to opportunities that come your way.

Location Freedom: Yes, you can have the ability to choose where you want to live, work, and spend your time, unrestricted by geographical boundaries. This concept has gained immense popularity, particularly with the rise of remote work and digital nomadism. In my experience, one of the benefits is work flexibility, allowing me to work from any place with an internet connection, including on a cruise ship. Whether it's a beach in Bali, a café in Paris, or your hometown, you can perform your job without being tied to a specific office or city. This flexibility can lead to a better work-life balance and increased job satisfaction. It can also provide you with cultural experiences by allowing you to choose to live in different parts of the world and exposing you to diverse cultures, languages, and lifestyles. You can enrich your life experience and broaden your perspective, making you more adaptable and open-minded.

Another aspect of location freedom is choosing places with a lower cost of living. For example, you might earn a salary based on the cost of living in a major city but choose to live in a more affordable location, thereby increasing your disposable income and savings. It has fostered my personal growth by exposing me to new environments and challenges, enhancing problem-solving skills, resilience, and independence. It also allows me to travel to freely assist my elderly mother.

You can also choose places that match your lifestyle preferences, such as locations with better climates, recreational activities, or healthcare, improving your quality of life and well-being. The ability to continuously travel and explore new destinations mainly appeals to those passionate about adventure. Additionally, location freedom enables you to be closer to family and friends scattered across different regions, allowing for more meaningful relationships. Professionally, it opens up opportunities to collaborate with international teams, attend global conferences, and tap into worldwide markets, expanding your career prospects.

Freedom of Association: You can decide who you surround yourself with, steering clear of negative influences and choosing those who uplift and inspire you. How and with whom we spend our time matters deeply and significantly impacts our wealth, quality of life, success, and goals. Research shows over and over that our need to belong and fit in with people around us is one of the most significant drivers in our lives. This freedom is crucial for personal growth, mental well-being, and overall life satisfaction. By associating with positive, supportive individuals, you can enhance your outlook on life, reduce stress, and foster a sense of belonging and security. It also facilitates professional development by connecting you with ambitious, knowledgeable, and driven individuals who can provide valuable advice and mentorship.

Distancing yourself from toxic relationships also protects you from negative influences hindering your progress. Building a network of like-minded, supportive people provides a safety net during tough times and enriches your social experiences, ultimately contributing to a higher quality of life. Exercising this freedom involves evaluating relationships, seeking out like-minded individuals, setting boundaries, being intentional about your associations, and investing in meaningful relationships. One of the keys to my success has been ensuring that I put myself in rooms with people who are part of a rising tide. I have coaches, mentors, and peers who continue to stretch and remind me of my goals and dreams.

Freedom of Purpose: Ultimately, freedom of purpose empowers me to live a life that is not just successful but also profoundly meaningful. I can pursue my true calling, engage in activities that bring me joy, and positively impact the world. This freedom allows me to align my life with my passions and values, creating deep fulfillment and satisfaction. When you are free to follow your purpose, you can dedicate your energy to endeavors that resonate with your core beliefs and interests, fostering a sense of meaning and direction in your life. This pursuit enhances your happiness and allows you to contribute positively to society, creating a ripple effect of good. By focusing on what truly matters, you can innovate, inspire, and uplift those around you, making a significant and lasting difference. Achieving this freedom involves introspection to identify your passions, the courage to follow your dreams, and the resilience to overcome obstacles. Where you pursue your true purpose, do what brings you joy, and positively impact the world. Recognizing and overcoming the excuses holding you back from living a truly wealthy life is essential.

I am grateful as I sit in my office, reflecting on my journey. I have built a life of education, stability, and purpose from being a teenage refugee with nothing. And while money was a significant part of that journey, the lessons and the spirit of perseverance made the difference. This journey allowed me to release any fear about money and step into the possibility of creating a money framework for helping women build their lives of abundance.

Today, I am dedicated to providing empowering content that educates, elevates, and inspires women to embrace their uniqueness, navigate the curves of their life journeys, and live their best lives while making the money they desire. My mission is to celebrate and uplift women from all walks of life to create influence, impact, and income.

At this point, I fully understood what money meant, far beyond its monetary value. I realized it was a tool for creating opportunities, a means to achieve security and freedom, and a catalyst for personal and professional growth. Embracing the right mindset, I saw opportunities arise from strategic thinking, careful planning, and a willingness to take calculated risks. Networking became crucial as I connected with like-minded individuals who shared insights and opened doors to new ventures. I harnessed positive energies, stayed focused and motivated, and became adept at yielding my money effectively through wise investments and financial decisions. This comprehensive understanding led me to write a framework detailing the principles and strategies that had transformed my approach to money, providing a roadmap for sustainable financial success and independence.

My Money Framework™ can transform your view, journey, and potential by comprehensively understanding money's true power and purpose. The word "money" itself encapsulates the essential elements of this transformation: M stands for Mindset, cultivating a positive and strategic approach to finances; O represents Opportunities, recognizing and seizing chances for growth and advancement; N signifies Networking, leveraging connections to enhance knowledge and open new doors; E stands for Energy, maintaining focus and motivation to drive success; and Y denotes Yield, effectively managing and multiplying your resources. Through my "Crowning the Money Queen™" 12-week coaching program, each letter of the Money Framework™ will take you on a transformative journey, empowering you to master your finances and achieve lasting financial independence and freedom.

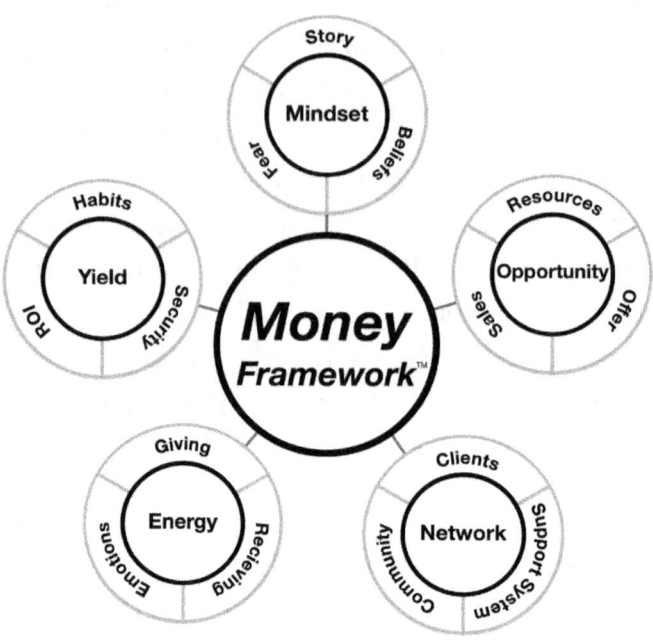

To begin your journey, I'm offering you a complimentary download to help you uncover how you can crown yourself as the ruler of your money.

https://keap.app/contact-us/8750217476947774

To join the waiting list for the next cohort of the "Crowning the Money Queen™" 12-week coaching program, use this link.

https://keap.app/contact-us/5379804610878245

Colleen K. Hendry

Founder of Virtual Run Co

https://www.linkedin.com/in/colleenkhendry/
https://www.facebook.com/colleen.k.hendry/
https://www.instagram.com/virtualrunco/
https://www.virtualrunco.com/

With almost twenty years of professional experience, Colleen has dedicated her career to pioneering forward-thinking technology solutions across diverse sectors such as security, healthcare, retail, and automotive. Her proficiency spans various domains including Product Management, Strategy, Branding, Sales, Training, Operations, Project Management, Pricing, Digital Technology, Artificial Intelligence, Machine Learning, Software as a Service (SaaS), and Mobile Application Development. Colleen boasts a track record of delivering over 16 successful mobile applications to market, complemented by numerous web-based applications. Additionally, she holds a patent for technology she actively contributed to developing.

Colleen is the author of the children's book, "*The Adventures of Kimchi and Pebbles: Learning Together*".

CREDIT CARDS UNLEASHED: HARNESSING WEALTH POTENTIAL

By Colleen K. Hendry

Credit cards are often viewed with apprehension, primarily due to their association with debt and overspending. However, when used responsibly and strategically, credit cards can be powerful tools for wealth accumulation. In this chapter, we will explore how to leverage credit cards to increase wealth, examining various strategies, tips, and considerations. In order to leverage credit cards as a wealth-growing tool, you will need to set yourself up for success. In this chapter, I will provide strategies that you can apply as well as some tips on how you can avoid bad credit card debt and reduce some of your apprehension.

Credit cards haven't always been good friends to me. I worked at the jewelry counter at JCPenney in high school. There were so many pretty things staring me in the face everyday. I was able to help women find just the right ring or earrings they were looking for. I sold countless engagement rings, which was always exciting. Being in retail, I was always in front of material things and coveting those who were able to buy them. I often stared at a freshwater pearl bracelet and earring set that I would try on every shift. On my 18th birthday, I applied for a JCPenney credit card. This was a right of passage as an 18 year old at the time. I was excited to be able to purchase all those pretty things, including that pearl set I'd had my eyes on for over a year.

My parents told me that was a good way to build my credit. It's funny—my parents instilled a lot of my neuroses around money that I still carry with me today. However, they never really showed me how to save or manage my money responsibly. My parents would talk about their thrift savings and work overtime and tell us it was for us kids. But I don't ever recall having a proactive conversation with them about what credit card debt could do. There may have been a passing conversation about not spending more than you can afford, but I knew everything at the time, since I was 18, right? There wasn't a lot instilled in me, which led to very irresponsible spending and a lot of debt. I was buying jewelry and clothes that I didn't really need as well as eating fast food for almost every meal. I don't know how much interest I paid over the years and I don't think I ever want to know.

Throughout my 20s and early 30s, I was drowning in credit card debt and interest. I was in way over my head and funding a lifestyle I couldn't afford. The way I reasoned it in my head was that I wouldn't get ahead if I didn't spend. And, I knew that I would continue to work hard to advance in my career, inevitably increasing my salary. I was funding my life in college, grad school, travel to other countries, and just basic living. I lived life and spent on experiences without thinking about how that might affect my future buying power.

While getting my MBA, I decided that I would get a consolidation loan. A consolidation loan would let me roll my tuition and credit card debt into one. The interest was much less. Now, this would have been a sound decision if I had stopped using credit cards. I still wasn't in the position to do that. I could barely afford the place I was living and I didn't want to miss out on experiences with my friends. I reasoned with myself that once I got my MBA, I would have the ability to advance in my career and start making the money I needed to make to live comfortably and pay off my debt.

All of this debt and interest made me focus on a strategy for how I was going to dig myself out of it. I didn't incur this debt overnight, so unless I won the lottery, I wasn't going to pay it off overnight. I was going to have to make those tough decisions of skipping a trip to Las Vegas with my friends or not buying that Tiffany's bracelet I really wanted. I wasn't going to totally deprive myself, but I was definitely going to focus on my strategy.

There are two key principles I applied. The first strategy was to build my savings. I am a firm believer that you need to have liquid cash, always. I am frugal in a lot of areas. I mentioned earlier that my parents didn't teach me well about credit cards. What they did instill in me, like most who grew up in the rural midwest, is that the floor can come out from underneath your feet at any time, so you better have money stashed away for a rainy day, just not in the mattress in case the house caves in.

You need to have money for those small emergencies that are inevitable. There are unforeseeable things that can be thrown at you out of nowhere on any given day and you need to be as prepared as possible. While I could have focused on only paying down my debt, I knew that if one of those unforeseeable things happened, I would then be in the "one step forward, two steps back" situation. If I didn't have money to pay for new tires, I would end up paying ten fold if I had to put them on my credit card. Having the cash available in parallel to making payments to reduce debt is extremely important. My rule of thumb was to have one month's salary in savings. That was money I could not touch for frivolous or daily expenses. That money was there to help with those unplanned events.

Once I had that one month salary, I would start taking the money I would put into savings and start using that for extra loan and credit card payments. Anything extra always went toward a payment to reduce my debt. I had one credit card that I would only use for emergencies or for those expenses that required a card, but I would pay that immediately that day or the next day. I did not wait until the end of the month because that would give me a false sense of how much money I really had.

Throughout my career, there have been times when I was able to expect some kind of annual bonus. Typically, I would also receive money back from taxes. Both of those were money I ignored. When I say ignore, I mean that I didn't get to spend that money on anything new. I would put some in savings and the rest went to pay off debt. Period. This was "free" money. It wasn't guaranteed and it was always a different amount. If you ever receive a lump sum of money, you need to pretend it doesn't exist. It needs to be put in savings or used to pay down debt. Hands down.

Once I was making money that was well above how I was living, I started strategizing and using all my extra money, bonuses, etc. to pay debt and slowly increase my savings to two months' salary. From the ages of 32–36, I was extremely diligent about taking any extra income and applying it to debt. If I received a raise at work, that extra money went toward paying off debt. One way to make this extra money a little easier to ignore was by having multiple bank accounts for paychecks. I would have a percentage put into my debt payment account and the rest went into my day-to-day checking account. Having that percentage put into a different account made it easier to ignore and think I had more money.

I became debt free by the age of 36. Debt free. I had no debt. The relief and sense of accomplishment was profound. Now I could truly start the next chapter.

I remember the day I paid off my undergraduate loan. That felt amazing! I finally had a big loan repaid. It gave me that feeling of accomplishment and fueled my motivation to keep going! In my adult life, I started running. I started with 5Ks and progressed to 10Ks and then half marathons. I'm a competitive person by nature, so I started taking on that perspective. This isn't a 5k, it's a half marathon. The next big conquest was going to be my MBA consolidation loan, the biggest debt I had, which was close to $100,000. During this time, I also had to focus on paying my car payment and daily bills. Before I paid off my MBA loan, I paid off my car and truck loans. Then, the day came where I was at the finish line of my half marathon. I made the last payment for my MBA consolidation loan. Once I clicked on the 'Submit' button and saw the zero dollar balance, I felt like I had won an Olympic event! The feeling of accomplishment was so gratifying. It took hard work, planning, diligence, and failures along the way, but it was worth every decision and sacrifice.

Now, I could start fresh. I had a clean slate. I had no debt and could start focusing on how I was going to build my wealth. I told myself that I would never ever get into debt like that again, no matter what.

With a clean slate, it was time for me to explore advanced strategies for harnessing the synergy between credit card rewards, cashback programs, and other loyalty initiatives to strategically grow my wealth. I want to share these with you so that you can also integrate some of these elements effectively, so you, too, can optimize your financial gains and enhance your overall wealth-building efforts.

I had several jobs where travel was a huge part of the job. I quickly learned that having the points and perks on hotels and airlines could help me travel more than I could afford to. Many of my colleagues and friends would always have the airline cards. I stayed in hotels so often that I started to realize that is where the true expense and variability came in. Airline prices will only go so high, but the variability of hotel rooms based on the time of year and destination could be drastically different. At that time, you could get hotels for anywhere from $99 to top of the line at $400. These days, it is definitely different. But, at any rate, if you are going to take a seven day vacation, you are definitely going to spend more than $1,000 on a hotel room. You could have an expensive flight for $800...you are still saving money if you go the route of the hotel credit card perks. There is a difference of $200. On the airlines, you can get first rate upgrades for your flights. For a long flight, that is awesome, right? If flying from Boston to LA, having that experience is pretty great…but it only lasts for six hours. And for some, that might be worth every penny. At hotels, you can use points for your stay and most likely get an upgrade or perks based on your status. Not only are you getting a free room, you are getting an upgrade for seven days as opposed to the 12-hour round trip flight time. Weigh the difference for what matters most to you. I have an AmEx and a Matercard. I prefer my AmEx, but it's not accepted everywhere.

So, let's get started. How do you start? First, you need to understand your wealth goals. Wealth goals aren't just monetary. What kind of lifestyle are you looking for?

The ONLY way credit cards can be used to grow your wealth is if you're able to pay off the balance before any interest is incurred. Today, there are some cards that have more than 30% interest. One missed payment or high balance rollover will set your strategy back. Each missed payment and interest exponentially sets you back and is no longer helping. You can only leverage this wealth strategy if you have the means to pay off the card. This will require you to be diligent. Are you willing to check your balance everyday? Are you willing to do a daily budget check? You don't have to go big or go home with the strategy. You can start small and grow. But no matter where you are in your financial journey, if you are going to apply this strategy, you need to be able to budget and pay your credit card off each month. One strategy that I have implemented is paying my card balance weekly. By doing this, I am diminishing the amount of interest I am getting in my bank account. I have determined, for me, that I am willing to incur this cost for peace of mind. I pay my balance off weekly so that I don't have "sticker shock" at the end of the month. Of course I know what I am spending during the month and am watching my budget, but it doesn't make it easier for me to swallow that big ticket monthly balance. If I pay off at the end of each week, then I am more at ease with the dollar amount. For my mental well-being, that small amount of money I didn't earn in interest is worth so much more. You choose what payment cycle works best for you and implement that. I do recommend that you always pay at least a few days before the due date. You never know what life is going to throw at you on the day it is due, so it's better to be proactive. The most important rule, regardless of the strategy, is the balance at the end of the month must always be 0. Again, if you can't have the balance be 0, this strategy is not for you. If you are not able to pay the card on time and have a late fee plus interest, you have ruined the strategy.

- Take Stock
- Research
- Implement

Take Stock

- Do an assessment of your current situation. Conducting an assessment will be critical to your strategy.
- Identify your goals and align your cards to that strategy.

Tips to Take Stock:

- How many credit cards do you have now?
  - o Do any of them have rewards, and are you optimizing those cards for the maximum benefits?
  - o Do you have cards that don't make sense anymore? Do you have cards that you aren't using?
    - Close those accounts.
    - Check your credit report to see if you have any open accounts that you forgot about and close those.
- Do you have a balance on any of your cards?
  - o Pay them off.
- What is the credit limit you can bear?

Tips for your Research

Research. Now it is up to you to research the cards and benefits that will meet your portfolio needs. You will want to diversify what you have in order to optimize all areas of your personal and professional life. The Motley Fool and NerdWallet websites have great comparisons and recommendations that can help you get started.

Begin by assessing your financial goals, spending patterns, and lifestyle preferences to develop a tailored rewards strategy. Consider the following factors:

- Reward Categories: Identify credit cards that offer rewards in categories aligned with your spending habits, such as groceries, dining, travel, or entertainment.

- Optimal Redemption Methods: Evaluate redemption options for each rewards program to determine the most valuable and cost-effective ways to utilize earned points or cashback.

- Synergy Between Programs: Look for opportunities to combine rewards from different sources to enhance your overall earning potential. For example, some loyalty programs allow you to transfer points to partner airlines or hotels, increasing redemption flexibility and value.

- Additional considerations

    o Cash back. Cash back cards are great because you are getting money back. But just cash back isn't going to bring you wealth. What you do with that cash back is going to be important. You definitely want to forget that cashback exists and invest it. We will discuss roundups and investments later in this chapter.

    o Travel. If you travel, look at past trips and future trips.

Determine your most frequent travel, your bucket list travel, etc. Once you have that mapped out, it is important to search those destinations to find out which hotels are there. For example, if you want to travel to St. John in the US Virgin Islands, a Hilton AmEx will not do you any good, since there are no Hilton properties on St. John. If you want to stay on St. John with points, a Marriott card will be what you need.

o Another key factor to look at here is the number of points it takes per night. You need to see the points per dollar you receive and determine how much money and usage of the card it will take to fund your seven day vacation. If it is something that isn't going to be attainable based on your spending, you might need to reconsider.

o Retailer Cards. Some of these cards can offer great benefits based on your personal or business spending. If you are a contractor, you would think that Lowe's would be the card that you want. But let's think about that. Sure, you can get a discount or savings based on the membership discounts. Is that going to be worth it in the long run? A lot of the things you purchase could be a write-off, so is that savings really saving you in the long run? Why not double dip and use an airline or hotel card on those large, everyday purchases so you can earn for your personal money through business spending? There are cards that provide you with higher cash back at their retail location. For example, Apple has a Mastercard that allows you to get cash back along with discounts on purchases at their store. There are several opportunities and promotions for higher percentages. For example, one month they may give 5% cashback at any grocery store you shop at.

o Cashback Plus. Cashback is great. But what you do with that cashback is going to be critical to your overall wealth. Cashback is essentially savings on your purchases. How do you make your savings work for you? Invest. Today, there are so many opportunities to invest the cashback immediately.

o Roundups. You can sign up for roundups to round up to the next dollar and put that money in a savings or investment account. Roundups are a great way to have that extra cash that you don't notice, and it adds up quickly. Some roundups have you deposit into a savings account, which is great if it is a high yield savings account. If it is an account that you can touch on a daily basis or incurs very little interest, it won't be a great long term strategy. You also want to make sure that the roundups are going to be available with your card. For example, an Apple Mastercard can't be connected to Acorns for roundups. Acorns was established in 2012 and has seen significant investors including Jennifer Lopez, Ashton Kutcher, and Kevin Durant, along with companies like PayPal and NBCUniversal. However, Apple has their own roundup, cashback that can be routed to their High Yield Savings Account (HYSA). Just make sure that you are doing all the research to make sure the card and investment strategies have synergies or it will be a wasted effort.

- Where you use your cards is also a strategy. You are now on the way to creating wealth and all your purchases need to align with that strategy. You should develop your short and long term goals and revisit them monthly to make sure you are on track. If not monthly, absolutely quarterly.

- For example, if you have a big trip coming up in a year, you may determine that all of your daily purchases should be done on your Hilton Amex. This could get you great upgrades during your trip and potentially get you a nicer room or additional perks. Or, you may be top tier status with enough points for a free stay and upgrade for your seven day stay. You may decide that for the next year you will be using your cash back credit card that has roundups invested in your HYSA so you have your excursion money saved and ready for your trip without even knowing it is there. Remember your status, though. If you need to spend a certain amount per year to keep your status and that is important to you, you might need to use your Hilton AmEx or a hybrid approach.

- If you choose to get a hotel credit card, that is the only card you should be using when you are staying at that hotel. If you have another that gives you 3% cash back, don't use it. Use the hotel credit card because of the extra points, number of stays required for status, etc. Limit your number of credit cards. For myself, I have two personal cards and one for my business. You want to get the most bang for your buck.

- Double dip whenever you get the chance! Double dipping is just like it sounds. Get the benefits for maximizing your benefits. There could be a promotion happening with one of your cards that gives 5% cash back with a hotel stay. You are staying at a Hilton property and using a Hilton AmEx. You are already getting points as a Hilton Diamond Member for the stay. Understand the number of points you will be getting for that stay. Then look at the number of additional points you will receive by putting it on AmEx. Once you have that, look at how 5% cash back compares. Then look at the additional money that would be invested or saved. If the cash back equates to a higher dollar value while not compromising your Hilton status, you should use that if it aligns with your goals. So now you are receiving points for your stay and cash back on your card that will be invested in your HYSA. You have just double dipped!

- Leveraging Loyalty Programs and Benefits. In addition to credit card rewards and cashback programs, loyalty initiatives offered by retailers, airlines, hotels, and other businesses can further enhance your wealth-building efforts. To leverage loyalty programs effectively:

  - Strategic Membership: Join loyalty programs for businesses you frequent regularly, maximizing earning potential and access to exclusive perks and discounts.

  - Status Benefits: Pursue elite status or tiered membership levels within loyalty programs to unlock additional benefits, such as priority service, complimentary upgrades, or enhanced rewards earning rates.

  - Pooling Points and Miles: Consolidate points and miles earned across various loyalty programs to achieve higher redemption thresholds and access premium rewards or experiences.

There are a lot of things you can do to slowly implement a plan depending on the stage of wealth you are at. Start small and grow or completely revamp and break out of the gate with heat!

Implement

Cash is king. We are hearing a lot of that in the news. A lot of small businesses, like your local nail salon or service work, use cash as an opportunity to provide lower prices and discounts.

Some businesses will even charge you a higher rate (i.e. 4%) to deter you from using your card which might give you 3% cash back. If you pay a 4% higher rate and use a card that gives you 3% or less cash back, you have spent more for the service. This might not always be a bad thing. In some instances, the 1% may not be significant. You have tied that 3% cash back to your investment account, so it will start making money for you. If you pay cash and save the 4%, will you put the 1% in your investment account to match what you would have been earning? Probably not. If the service doesn't incur additional fees for using your credit card, use it. This is going to build your points or get you cash back with the opportunity to invest.

Maximize your category bonuses. In most cases, credit cards will offer different promotions or category bonuses. Some may offer double, triple, or even quintuple points in different categories. For example, AmEx Gold Card offers four Membership Rewards points per dollar at US supermarkets (on up to $25,000 per calendar year in purchases, then one point per dollar).

Some small things you can do to increase your purchases without a cost to you is dinner out with friends. If you are out to dinner, offer to pay and have others pay you through one of the many apps out there.

Tracking, Optimization, and Even More Benefits.

Maintaining a systematic approach to tracking your rewards, cashback earnings, and loyalty program benefits is essential for effective optimization. Utilize digital tools, spreadsheets, or dedicated apps to monitor your progress, track expiration dates, and identify opportunities for further optimization. I am old school and use Excel to track all of my finances. I have customized spreadsheets with pivot tables and graphs. If you do a Google search for "personal finance tracker app," you will get a lot of recommendations.

Here are even more benefits from having a strongly executed strategy for paying off your credit card balance(s) each month.

Avoiding Interest Charges: Perhaps the most obvious benefit of paying off your credit cards each month is that you avoid accruing interest charges. Credit cards typically have high interest rates, often ranging from 15% to 25% or more annually. By paying off your balance in full before the due date, you effectively eliminate any interest charges on your purchases.

Saving Money: Since you're not paying interest on your credit card balances, you save money in the long run. This saved money can be redirected toward other financial goals, such as savings, investments, or paying down debt with higher interest rates.

Maintaining Control of Your Finances: Paying off your credit cards in full each month allows you to stay in control of your finances. You avoid the burden of carrying over debt from one month to the next, which can lead to stress and financial instability.

Preserving Credit Score: Your credit utilization ratio, which is the amount of credit you're using compared to your total available credit, plays a significant role in determining your credit score. By paying off your credit cards every month, you keep your credit utilization low, which can positively impact your credit score.

Building Strong Credit History: Consistently paying off your credit card balances demonstrates responsible financial behavior to credit bureaus. This helps build a positive credit history, which is essential for accessing favorable loan terms, mortgages, and other financial opportunities in the future.

Maximizing Rewards and Benefits: Many credit cards offer rewards and benefits, such as cash back, points, miles, or other perks. By paying off your balances every month, you can fully capitalize on these rewards without negating their value through interest charges.

Avoiding Debt Accumulation: Paying off your credit cards in full each month prevents the accumulation of debt. High levels of credit card debt can quickly spiral out of control, leading to financial hardship, strained relationships, and diminished quality of life.

Peace of Mind: Knowing that you don't carry credit card debt from month to month can provide peace of mind and reduce financial stress. You can focus on other aspects of your life and financial goals without the weight of debt hanging over you.

In summary, paying off your credit cards in full every month offers numerous benefits, including saving money on interest, maintaining control of your finances, preserving your credit score, maximizing rewards, and enjoying peace of mind. It's a sound financial habit that contributes to long-term financial stability and wealth building. One of the most important things to remember during your half marathon is that there will be stops and injuries along the way. What I mean by that is it's okay to have a set back. You can and will come back from it. You will finish the race if you are mindful and get back to the track.

Using a credit card instead of a debit card offers several advantages, including:

Fraud Protection: Credit cards typically offer stronger fraud protection compared to debit cards. With credit cards, you're not liable for fraudulent charges as long as you report them promptly. Debit cards, on the other hand, may have more limited liability protections, and fraudulent transactions can directly impact your bank account balance.

Building Credit History: Responsible use of a credit card can help establish and build your credit history. Credit card issuers report your payment history to credit bureaus, which influences your credit score. A positive credit history is essential for accessing favorable loan terms, mortgages, and other financial opportunities in the future.

Convenience and Flexibility: Credit cards offer greater convenience and flexibility in managing your finances. They can be used for online purchases, travel reservations, and other transactions where debit cards may not be accepted or may have limitations, such as rental car reservations and hotel bookings.

Grace Period: Credit cards come with a grace period, usually between 20 to 30 days, during which you can pay off your balance without incurring interest charges. This provides temporary financing for your purchases and allows you to manage your cash flow more effectively. Debit card transactions are immediately deducted from your bank account, offering less flexibility in timing your payments.

Purchase Protection: Many credit cards offer purchase protection, which covers eligible purchases against damage, theft, or loss for a certain period after the purchase date. This additional layer of security can provide peace of mind when making significant purchases.

Travel Benefits: Certain credit cards offer travel-related benefits, such as travel insurance, rental car insurance, airport lounge access, and waived foreign transaction fees. These perks can save you money and enhance your travel experience compared to using a debit card.

Overall, using a credit card offers several benefits over a debit card, including enhanced fraud protection, the opportunity to build credit history, rewards and benefits, convenience and flexibility, a grace period for payments, emergency funding, purchase protection, and travel benefits. However, it's important to use credit cards responsibly and to avoid overspending in order to reap these benefits effectively.

Conclusion

My hope in writing this chapter is that you will start training for your big race like I did. Being financially independent is such an amazing feeling. The opportunities for you grow exponentially the more you grow your wealth. I hope the strategies I have shared about integrating rewards, cash back, and loyalty programs offer a powerful means of strategically growing your wealth. By crafting a comprehensive rewards strategy, maximizing cashback opportunities, and leveraging loyalty initiatives effectively, you can optimize your financial gains and achieve your long-term financial objectives like I have. With careful planning, disciplined execution, and ongoing optimization, you can harness the full potential of integrated wealth-building strategies to secure a brighter financial future. Now, lace up those sneakers and go the distance!

Prudence Hatchett

PH Counseling, LLC
Owner & Mental Wellness Specialist

https://www.facebook.com/phcounselingllc
https://www.phcounseling.orghttps://learn-with-
prudence.myshopify.com/

Prudence Hatchett has over 17 years of combined experience in the mental health and educational fields. She earned a BA in Psychology and an M.S. in Special Education from Mississippi State University, and M.Ed. in Counselor Education from the University of Mississippi. She is a National Certified Counselor, Licensed Professional Counselor & Board Qualified Supervisor, and a Board-Certified Coach. She has specialized certifications in anxiety, grief, substance abuse, and Autism. She holds a master's level AA educator's license with educational endorsements in the areas of Guidance Counseling, Mild/Moderate Disabilities, Emotional Disability, and Psychology. Prudence is a business professional with her own private practice, "PH Counseling, LLC", and her own ecommerce store & brand, "Learn with Prudence." Prudence supports people in nourishing their mental health and emotional wellness through the power of education, strength exploration, skill building, and elevating confidence

BALANCING THE SCALES: LEVERAGING MONEY AND MENTAL HEALTH

By Prudence Hatchett

As I dive deeper into my chosen career path, the subject of money is often front and center and one I can not ignore. Whether it's deciding on a price point for my services, creating a payment plan with my clients, or just routine budgeting for my own personal bills and household demands, money is woven into my everyday life. Currently, I am much more comfortable with not only talking about money, but asking for the money that better correlates with my service options. Please notice that I said, "Currently, I am much more comfortable," because this was not always the case.

I remember when I was a teenager working at my first minimum wage job, I was ecstatic at the idea of receiving my own paycheck that I could cash at the bank. I considered that to be my first step toward adulthood. Although it's considered common knowledge that we all need money to live and survive, something magical happened when I got my first check. It was a very powerful moment in my world. Honestly, receiving my own money felt pretty good! It felt good to utilize my own money to buy myself something and to provide for myself, and I started to crave the freedom that came along with the independence of having my own money. Fast forward to today, my career in entrepreneurship has helped transform my view and relationship with money for the better.

Although the feeling of having money felt magical, talking about it did not feel as magical. Discussing money can be tricky because everyone, including friends and family, has their own ideas, which may or may not align with yours. When the latter happens, we typically tend to shy away from the subject and maybe just accept the normal ideals about money, which are usually steeped in family or cultural traditions. Unfortunately, in some cultures, the idea of wanting "more money" may be frowned upon, or maybe even viewed as un-lady-like.

Money is an essential part of life and a resource that must be handled with care and dignity if we want to take full advantage of its rightful potential. With advances in technology, entrepreneurship on the rise, and women creating a lane for themselves, the need for financial literacy is at an all time high. I am honored to be contributing to a book of this nature because it opens the channels of communication about money, highlights the increased interests between women and money, and encourages financial confidence.

Women and Money

In most daily routines, whether single or in a partnership, women often have many responsibilities. They balance being caregivers, earning money, and managing the household. If not careful, this balancing act can negatively impact their mental health, leaving little room for self-care and personal development. However, despite all these demands, paying attention to money matters is still very important, because money can positively affect a person's quality of life. Unfortunately, the subject of money is often overlooked, undervalued, and misunderstood.

Throughout history, learning about personal finances was not always an immediate concern for most women. Let's be honest; this is mainly due to traditional gender roles. Nonetheless, it was and is still significant in shaping their lives. Understanding personal finance equips women with the tools to navigate the complexities of financial decision-making, therefore empowering them to take control of their economic futures. Moreover, developing sound money management skills has the potential to not only enhance their financial security but also to positively contribute to their mental health by increasing self-confidence, lessening financial anxiety, and creating independence.

Financial literacy grants women the ability to make informed choices regarding budgeting, saving, investing, and debt management. This newfound knowledge instills a sense of confidence and autonomy, empowering them to take charge of their financial circumstances and create a more sustainable future. By understanding their financial options and taking proactive steps to manage their finances, women can alleviate the mental burden often associated with financial instability.

Furthermore, financial literacy enables women to participate more effectively in the workforce. Equipped with the necessary skills and knowledge, they can negotiate salaries, plan for retirement, and make informed decisions about their careers. This newfound economic empowerment translates into increased self-worth, improved job satisfaction, and enhanced mental well-being.

In a world in which gender disparities persist, financial literacy becomes a crucial tool for women to bridge the economic gender gap. By arming themselves with financial knowledge, women can break free from the traditional roles and stereotypes that have historically limited their economic opportunities. This newfound financial independence empowers them to make choices that align with their personal goals and aspirations, ultimately fostering a new sense of self-fulfillment and purpose.

Noteworthy Statistics

Several interesting facts regarding women, money, and mental health:

1. The gender pay gap significantly affects women's mental health. Studies have shown that women who experience wage disparities report higher levels of stress and anxiety compared to men. The chronic stress associated with earning less for the same work can lead to long-term mental health issues such as

depression and anxiety disorders. *Source: American Psychological Association. "Stress in America: Paying with Our Health." 2015.*

2. Financial abuse is a common form of domestic violence that disproportionately affects women. It involves controlling a woman's ability to acquire, use, and maintain financial resources. Victims of financial abuse often suffer from significant mental health issues, including depression, anxiety, and post-traumatic stress disorder (PTSD). The abuse can lead to long-term financial instability and reliance on the abuser, exacerbating mental health problems. *National Coalition Against Domestic Violence. "Financial Abuse Fact Sheet." 2019.*

3. Women often shoulder a disproportionate amount of unpaid labor, such as caregiving and household chores. This "invisible" work contributes to financial inequality and increased stress, which negatively impacts mental health. The burden of unpaid labor can lead to burnout, reduced career opportunities, and a higher incidence of mental health issues like depression. *Oxfam International. "Why unpaid care work matters for women's economic empowerment and mental health." 2018.*

4. Women who face workplace discrimination, including sexual harassment and gender bias, report higher levels of mental health problems. The stress and trauma from such experiences can result in conditions such as anxiety, depression, and PTSD. Moreover, the fear of retaliation or job loss often prevents women from reporting these issues, perpetuating a cycle of abuse and mental health deterioration. *Equal Employment Opportunity Commission. "Select Task Force on the Study of Harassment in the Workplace." 2016.*

5. Single mothers are particularly vulnerable to financial stress, which significantly impacts their mental health. They often

experience high levels of financial strain due to single-income households, which can lead to chronic stress, anxiety, and depression. The pressure of balancing work, childcare, and financial responsibilities without adequate support exacerbates these mental health challenges. *Pew Research Center. "Parenting in America: Outlook, worries, aspirations are strongly linked to financial situation." 2015.*

But there is hope.........

6. Economic empowerment, including financial independence and literacy, has a positive impact on women's mental health. Women who have control over their finances tend to experience lower levels of stress and higher levels of self-esteem and life satisfaction. Financial literacy programs targeting women have been effective in improving both financial stability and mental well-being. *World Health Organization. "Women's empowerment and their mental health: a review of evidence and a future research agenda." 2017.*

Although most of the statistics above are on the negative side, point number six leads us to renewed hope in financial resiliency. As women are starting to collectively pay more attention and get involved with financial education to enhance their own lives, women have a direct impact on enhancing the future workforce. It is important for women to learn about financial literacy for several key reasons:

Financial Independence: Understanding money management helps women achieve financial independence, allowing them to support themselves without relying on others.

1. Economic Empowerment: Financial literacy empowers women to make informed decisions about investments, savings, and spending, which can improve their overall economic status.

2. Security and Stability: Knowledge of personal finance provides women with the tools to plan for the future, including retirement, emergencies, and unforeseen expenses, ensuring greater financial security and stability.

3. Equal Opportunities: Learning about money can help bridge the gender pay gap and ensure women are equally represented in financial decision-making processes, both personally and professionally.

4. Confidence and Control: Financial literacy boosts confidence and gives women control over their economic situations, reducing stress and enhancing their ability to achieve personal and professional goals.

5. Protection Against Financial Abuse: Understanding finances can help women recognize and protect themselves against financial abuse, ensuring they maintain control over their resources.

6. Role Modeling: Financially knowledgeable women can serve as role models for their families and communities, promoting financial literacy and responsible money management across generations.

In summary, financial education is crucial for women to gain independence, security, confidence, and equality in both their personal and professional lives.

Multiple Skills, Multiple Streams

Creating multiple streams of income involves developing various sources of revenue, which can enhance financial security and stability. Instead of relying solely on a single paycheck, women can diversify their earnings by exploring different opportunities. This can include working a primary job while engaging in side gigs or freelance work, and investing in stocks, real estate, or other assets that generate passive income. Starting a business, whether large or small, brick-and-mortar or online ventures, is a proven method for women gaining financial independence. Additionally, leveraging skills and hobbies can lead to income through consulting, tutoring, or selling handmade goods. By having multiple income streams, women can reduce financial risk, increase savings, and achieve greater financial flexibility and independence. This strategy not only provides a safety net in case one source of income is disrupted, but also opens up potential for wealth accumulation and financial growth over time.

Increasing skill competence plays a vital role in creating multiple streams of income by enabling individuals to diversify their capabilities and seize various opportunities. As women enhance their expertise in different areas, they can tap into multiple income sources such as freelance work, consulting, or entrepreneurial ventures. For example, a professional who develops skills in interior design, writing, and social media marketing can offer services in each field, thus generating revenue from diverse clients and projects.

Additionally, advanced skill sets can lead to the creation of passive income streams, such as writing ebooks, creating online courses, or developing software applications. By continuously learning and expanding their skills and interest, women not only increase their marketability but also reduce the risk associated with relying on a single source of income, thereby achieving greater financial stability and growth.

Passive income is money earned with minimal active involvement, allowing women to generate revenue without continuous effort or time investment. The primary advantage of passive income is that it provides financial stability and freedom, enabling individuals to build wealth over time without being tied to a regular job or specific working hours. This type of income can supplement regular earnings, contribute to retirement savings, and offer a buffer against economic uncertainties.

Entrepreneurship and Mental Health

Entrepreneurship and mental health are closely intertwined, as the unique demands and pressures of starting and running a business can significantly impact an entrepreneur's psychological well-being. Entrepreneurs often face high levels of stress and anxiety due to the uncertainty and risks associated with running a business. This includes financial instability, workload pressures, and the constant need to make critical decisions. Entrepreneurs frequently struggle with maintaining a healthy work-life balance. The intense dedication required to build a business can lead to long working hours, neglect of personal relationships, and inadequate self-care, which can exacerbate mental health issues.

The entrepreneurial journey can be lonely, as many entrepreneurs work in isolation, especially in the early stages of their ventures. This lack of social support can contribute to feelings of loneliness and depression. The relentless pursuit of business goals can lead to burnout, characterized by physical and emotional exhaustion, decreased motivation, and a sense of detachment. Burnout can severely impact an entrepreneur's ability to function effectively and maintain their business.

On the positive side, entrepreneurship can also foster resilience and strong coping skills. The challenges faced by entrepreneurs often require them to develop problem-solving abilities, adaptability, and perseverance, which can enhance their overall mental toughness. Building a robust support system is crucial for entrepreneurs. This includes seeking mentorship, joining entrepreneurial networks, and finding a community of like-minded individuals who understand the unique challenges of entrepreneurship. Professional mental health support, such as therapy or coaching, is beneficial for building and maintaining a sense of overall life balance.

Incorporating mindfulness practices and self-care routines into daily life can help entrepreneurs manage stress and maintain mental well-being. Regular exercise, meditation, positive hobbies, and ensuring adequate rest are essential components of a healthy lifestyle. Increasing awareness about the importance of mental health in entrepreneurship can lead to better support structures and resources for entrepreneurs. Education on recognizing the signs of mental health issues and knowing when to seek help is vital. Balancing the demands of the business with personal well-being, seeking support, and practicing self-care are essential strategies for maintaining mental health in the entrepreneurial journey.

Financial education is a powerful form of self-care that can significantly enhance one's overall well-being. Just as physical health is maintained through exercise and proper nutrition, financial health is nurtured through understanding and managing money effectively. By learning about budgeting, saving, investing, and debt management, women can reduce financial stress and anxiety, leading to a more stable and secure life. This knowledge empowers people to make informed decisions, achieve their financial goals, and prepare for unexpected expenses, thereby fostering a sense of control and peace of mind. Prioritizing financial literacy is not just about wealth accumulation; it's about investing in oneself, ensuring long-term security, and promoting mental and emotional health through financial stability.

Financial literacy is a vital tool that connects directly to achieving personal life goals. For women, effectively managing money can transform dreams into reality, whether those dreams involve buying a home, traveling, starting a business, or ensuring a comfortable retirement. Understanding how to create a budget and a savings plan allows women to accumulate the funds needed for a down payment on a house or care, which can provide a sense of stability and ownership. Smart money management also opens up the possibility of exploring the world, as strategic saving and investing can fund travel adventures with friends and family without financial strain.

For aspiring entrepreneurs, financial literacy is crucial in starting and sustaining a successful business. From managing startup costs to understanding cash flow, learning about money can be a powerful tool for creating the life you want. Finally, by planning and investing for the future, women can build a secure retirement fund, ensuring they can enjoy their later years without financial worries. In essence, financial literacy empowers women to take control of their finances and confidently pursue their life goals, turning aspirations into achievable milestones.

Women and Self-Trust

Women can learn to trust themselves more by cultivating a sense of positive self-awareness, building on their strengths, and celebrating their achievements. Self-awareness involves understanding one's values, skills, and limitations, which helps in making informed and confident decisions. By acknowledging and developing their unique strengths, women can reinforce their self-belief and reduce self-doubt. Setting and achieving small, manageable goals provides a sense of accomplishment and reinforces trust in one's abilities. Additionally, seeking out supportive networks and mentors can offer encouragement and validation, further boosting confidence. Overcoming challenges and learning from experiences, rather than fearing failure, can also strengthen self-trust. Ultimately, trusting oneself comes from a combination of self-knowledge, continuous personal growth, and the positive reinforcement of one's capabilities and successes.

Women can trust themselves with money more by educating themselves about personal finance, setting clear financial goals, and tracking their progress. Financial education, whether through books, online courses, or workshops, equips women with the knowledge and skills needed to make informed decisions about budgeting, saving, and investing. Setting specific, achievable financial goals provides a clear roadmap and purpose, making it easier to stay motivated and disciplined.

Regularly tracking income, expenses, and savings helps women understand their financial situation and make adjustments as needed, building confidence in their ability to manage money effectively. Additionally, seeking advice from financial mentors or joining financial literacy groups can provide support and validation. By taking these proactive steps, women can develop a strong sense of financial competence and trust in their money management skills, empowering them to achieve financial independence and security.

Barriers to self-trust for women can stem from societal expectations, cultural norms, and personal experiences. From a young age, women may internalize messages that undermine their confidence and self-belief, such as stereotypes about their abilities or societal pressures to prioritize others' needs over their own. Gender biases in education, workplaces, and leadership roles can also negatively impact women's confidence and contribute to imposter syndrome, where they doubt their accomplishments and fear being exposed as frauds. Additionally, experiences of discrimination, harassment, or gender-based violence can shatter women's trust in themselves and their ability to navigate the world safely.

Moreover, systemic inequalities, such as the gender pay gap and lack of access to resources and opportunities, can reinforce feelings of inadequacy and self-doubt. These barriers create a complex web of challenges that women must navigate in order to develop and maintain trust in themselves and their capabilities. Overcoming these barriers requires challenging societal norms, building supportive communities, and empowering women to recognize and celebrate their worth and potential.

Assessing Financial Skills

Women can assess their own money skills by taking a holistic approach that involves reflection, self-assessment, and seeking feedback. Firstly, reflecting on past financial decisions and behaviors can provide valuable insights into strengths and areas for improvement. This involves considering how well they have managed budgets, saved for goals, invested, and navigated financial challenges. Self-assessment involves honestly evaluating knowledge and abilities related to personal finance, such as budgeting, investing, debt management, and financial goal-setting. Women can identify areas where they feel confident and competent, as well as areas where they may need to learn more or seek support.

Seeking feedback from trusted sources, such as financial advisors, mentors, or peers, can offer valuable perspectives and insights into strengths and areas for growth. By combining reflection, self-assessment, and feedback, women can gain a comprehensive understanding of their money skills and take proactive steps to enhance their financial literacy and confidence.

Balancing the Scales: Leveraging Money and Mental Health

I developed this chapter to explore the connection between money and mental health. It's crucial to understand how these two areas are intertwined and how they can impact each other, both positively and negatively. I want you to pay close attention to the financial behavior tips below, and reflect on your own experiences of how you have managed your finances and mental health. Self-reflection is a proven practice that will help you become more self-aware of your behaviors, intentions, and goals. When we are more self-aware of our own behaviors, intentions, and goals, we can make better plans to create positive changes in our lives and secure a more financially stable future. I encourage you to practice these financial behaviors on a routine basis (i.e. daily or weekly), so that over time they will become financial habits. You must practice consistently for them to become a lifestyle.

1. Create a habit of saving. Of course, this behavior is one that does not come by surprise. However, in my experience, people can get caught up in the "rules" of saving and leave no room for flexibility in how they save. For example, if one can not save 10% out of their check this week like they have been advised to do, they may forgo saving altogether for the week. I encourage you to be consistent but flexible. For example, for one week you may be able to save 10%, but another week 25% or 1%.

2. Create a habit of budgeting. Knowing where your money is going and what you are spending it on is one of the best financial behaviors you can practice. This increases self-awareness, which will help you make better decisions, and you will understand which "money moves" are working and which aren't and adjust accordingly.

3. Secure your financial accounts. Secure all of your devices and documents with financially sensitive material (account numbers, passwords, security questions, etc.). In fact, don't be afraid to use some sort of lockbox for your important papers.

4. Live below your financial means to gain a certain lifestyle. Meaning, do not spend every dime you have every month. Of course, this is meant within reason, because I do understand inflation or not being paid enough for your work, or being paid just enough to make ends meet. If you can make some adjustments such as short term financial sacrifices (i.e. delayed gratification), you can create a financial cushion, giving yourself a soft place to land at the end of the month.

5. Live within your financial means to sustain a certain lifestyle. Meaning, try not to overspend or financially exert yourself. There should be a healthy balance between how much money

you have and how much money you bring in, and you should always be aware of how much money is going out.

6. Create a mindset of living in financial peace within yourself. Trust that you can learn financial literacy, identify financial stressors and responsibilities, and plan out your financial obligations accordingly.

7. When allowing someone to borrow money from you, create a repayment plan with the intended party. This helps create a timeline of paying the money back, which will help all parties have realistic expectations.

8. It's ok to like the idea of having money and wanting more of it. Things we genuinely like, we tend to nurture and take care of. Things we loath, we tend to misuse and emotionally abuse.

9. Try to do some good with your money, such as making donations, monetary or tangible. Surprise someone by paying a reasonable bill for them or sending a meal to their home. This could be something you do once every few months or every month if your heart desires. But please remember, this should not cause a financial burden, this should be reasonable and fall within your financial means.

10. Our financial habits often reflect our thought processes. This is why our beliefs and attitudes about money are so important. What we say and think about money becomes reinforced over time, shaping either a positive or negative mindset toward it.

    a. Reflect on these common negative thoughts about money and consider how they have impacted your financial attitude:

       i.   I am so broke.
       ii. I will never have enough money.

iii. I hate working.

iv. I hate paying bills.

b. Repeat these affirmations to positively reinforce your financial relationship and attitude towards money. Think of it as applying the "law of attraction."

i. I will learn to manage my money well and create a sense of financial peace.

ii. I will seek out financial literacy and increase my self-confidence about my money management skills.

iii. I like practicing self-awareness to identify where my money is going. It helps me feel in control.

iv. I will live within my financial means to live a comfortable life and create a more secure financial future.

Attracting Abundance

Women can become "money magnets" by adopting a mindset of abundance, cultivating financial literacy, and taking proactive steps to attract wealth and opportunities. Embracing an abundance mindset involves believing in one's worthiness to receive financial abundance and recognizing that opportunities for wealth creation are abundant. This mindset shift can help women overcome limiting beliefs and fears around money, allowing them to attract wealth with confidence and positivity. Cultivating financial literacy is essential for understanding how to manage money effectively, including budgeting, saving, investing, and building passive income streams.

By continuously learning and improving financial knowledge and skills, women can make informed decisions and leverage opportunities to grow and sustain wealth. Finally, taking proactive steps such as setting clear financial goals, investing in oneself and one's future, and surrounding oneself with supportive networks and mentors can help women become magnets for money and success. By aligning their mindset, knowledge, and actions with their financial goals, women can attract abundance and create the life of prosperity they desire.

Prudence Hatchett

Nichica F Melton, M.Ed

Coach and CEO of What She Said Coaching

https://www.instagram.com/nichicafmelton
www.nichicamelton.com

Meet Nichica F. Melton: a dynamic force of inspiration and empowerment. With a Bachelor's in Communication Studies and a Master's in Education Administration, Nichica's academic prowess is just the beginning. As a four-time published author, including her latest, "Cut the BS! 7 Simple Strategies To Unlock Higher Productivity," she's transforming lives one page at a time. Nichica's influence spans ministry, entrepreneurship, and real estate, where she ignites growth and prosperity. Whether speaking at events nationwide or coaching entrepreneurs to success, Nichica's passion shines through. As a wife and mother of 6, she's a beacon of faith, resilience, and unwavering dedication, guiding others on their journey to greatness. Connect with Nichica at www.nichicamelton.com and embark on a transformative adventure today.

HOW TO CREATE MONEY GENERATING AND SUSTAINING GOALS

By Nichica F Melton, M.Ed

In this chapter I am going to be discussing some simple strategies that will assist you in creating money-generating and money-sustaining goals. What I have found is that in many instances, the goals that we create or the activities that we do, do not align with the financial goals that we have established for ourselves, for our businesses, or for our families. Now please note that although these strategies may be labeled one, two, three, and four, that doesn't mean that I am giving them to you in order of importance. Some of the strategies you may already be doing and some of them may be new to you. If you're already doing a version of the strategy, tweak what you're doing to exactly what I'm saying in this chapter and see the difference it will make in your financial progress.

Strategy #1: Creating Long Term and Short Term Financial Goals

It is not enough to say that you want to make a certain amount of money for the year. For example, some people say they want to make six figures. You have to understand that six figures starts at $100,000 and ends at $999,999. Where are you trying to be on that spectrum? What is feasible for you based on where you are in your business now? Here's an exercise that I want you to do. Get out a piece of paper. At the top of the paper you're going to write the words, "Financial Goal for Year ___" (and put the year in there). Now I want you to put a dollar amount on the next line. The number that you just put is your safety number. It's the number that you feel comfortable with, and after doing some thinking, you feel like it's feasible for you to accomplish.

A successful business owner can never rest in the lane of being comfortable. You have to spend time being uncomfortable, because that means that you are being pushed and you are being stretched. What I want you to do is put an X through that number and then double it. That's right. I want you to double it because this is the amount that's going to push you. This is the amount that's going to require you to stay focused on your goals and your activities. You're not going to be able to slack off. You're not going to be able to make excuses. Now this goal is your annual goal, what you want to make for the year. The mistake that so many people make is taking that number and dividing it by 12 and then thinking that this is what they have to make every month. Well, what I want you to understand is that you have to build your foundation. If you are new to the business and you think that you're going to make that dollar amount in your first month of trying, maybe you will, but probably you won't. Why? Because you have not fully developed the skills and the activities that are required to make that dollar amount.

If you are a seasoned business owner and you are trying to make that amount in your next month, there may be some personnel changes that need to be made and possibly some policies and procedures that need to be adjusted. Don't make the assumption that just because you have been in business for a while, you know all that needs to be done in order to produce your next level of success. So what you have to do next is ask yourself what activities are required of you and your team, if you have one, in order to make that amount and get to the end result of the dollar amount that's at the top of your page. The key is figuring out what your goals are for each month, week, and day. Then, based on your goals, what are the activities that are required for your particular type of business to get to those goals? What do these activities look like on a daily basis? Make sure that they will produce the outcome (goals) that you have written down. How do I do that? You ask. Very good question. That leads us to Strategy #2.

Strategy #2: Creating SMART Goals for the Month, the Week, and the Day.

Just in case you are not familiar, SMART is an acronym that stands for Specific, Measurable, Achievable, Relevant, and Time Bound. What this means is that you can't just put down a random goal that doesn't align with anything and think that you are going to be successful in your business. Yes, you may accomplish the goal, but was that goal relevant to your overall goal for your business? Or was it just a task that you created to make yourself feel like you accomplished something?

So, let's start by working through an example of a SMART goal both for your personal and for your professional worlds.

Personal:

- Not SMART Goal: "I want to lose five pounds by the end of the month."

- SMART Goal: "I am going to workout for 30 minutes a day doing a DVD or YouTube workout video. I will do 50 jumping jacks, 15 burpees, 10 pushups, and 25 crunches every single day, Monday through Friday, in the morning before work, and on Saturday and Sunday, I rest."

The SMART goal is specific, measurable, achievable, relevant, and time-bound. Just saying you want to lose five pounds this month is leaving your goal to life and chance.

Professional:

So, let's look at the SMART framework within different types of businesses. Let's go with a home-based business. Let's say you're selling cosmetics, shirts, cookware, candles, or something along those lines. And you say for your goal that you want to profit $2,500 in month one because you want to build your momentum. Well, then you need to break that goal down into different parts.

For instance, if you're selling cosmetics, how many lipsticks, eye shadows, blushes, facial moisturizers, etc. do you need to sell in a month? Then break that down even further. How many appointments do you need to have? The numbers say that if you book five appointments, only two of them are going to happen. So if you only have five appointments for the month, you're not going to meet the goal. You need to look at booking five appointments a day and work up to that point. It may not happen consistently in the beginning.

So then the next thing is, how long does it take me to book five appointments? You probably don't know that right now, but this is building your system and your processes because once you know how long it takes for you to book five appointments a day, then you know how long you have to be on the phone every single day calling, texting, sliding into those DMs, and emailing. This is building your processes and helping you get to those SMART goals.

So, once you know the numbers, and it may take you a week to figure out the numbers, you can create your SMART goal. It may look something like, "I am going to make $2,500 this month by having a minimum of five face-to-face, virtual, or phone appointments a day. I will do this by spending an hour each day on the phone talking to people Monday-Friday from 6 pm–7 pm and Saturday from 11 am– noon and selling X number of products by the end of the month."

Now, if you're somebody who has an automated system, meaning that you have some type of CRM or system that will help you automate sending out emails and text messages to your clients, that's absolutely awesome. You gotta make sure you're using it. If you don't have the money for that right now, that's cool too. Don't down yourself or automatically kill your goal because you don't have that yet. That can definitely be a long term goal.

If you don't have a CRM and you don't have anyone helping you, then you have to make sure your day is properly prioritized so that you can send out the DMS and text messages and be on the phone in order to get your five appointments for the day. This is your first month: figuring out your processes and getting your momentum built up. This is how it works in sales, period. You've got to start somewhere and build that momentum. Then you start tweaking. Now, if you have an in-house assistant or VA who can go into the DMs for you or send the text messages for you, or you have that CRM, then you can constantly feed it, but you still have to get new clients. So set your goals based on the systems and processes that are and are not in place and you will build your momentum from there so that you can make the goals for months two, three, four, etc.

If you already have an established business, whether you have had success or not, you also would need to look at what you currently have in place. This includes your staff, your systems, your technology, everything. One thing feeds into the next, one thing supports the next, and you need to look at whether or not you have the right people in the right places. A lot of times we put people in positions based on their previous experience on their resume. However, we don't pay attention to what they're naturally gifted at. Pay attention to your people. Talk to your supervisors and your managers. Do you have the right people in the right places? Start there. Then look at your technology. Is your technology up to date, or is your technology beyond what your current staff is able to handle? The two have to be in alignment. When was the last time you reviewed your current systems? Not the technology aspect, but looking at your policies, your procedures, your systems that hold everything together and push everything forward. When is the last time they have been evaluated by somebody who actually does what you want to do? Not the arbitrary person behind the desk who has no clue and is only paying attention to the numbers. It needs to be a person who has accomplished what you are trying to accomplish. Someone that can mentor you into your next level of success.

Strategy #3: It Takes Money to Make Money

We have all heard this phrase before, and the saying is true. What I want you to understand is that not every door that opens is a door that you should walk through. You have to make sure that what you are getting ready to spend your money on is feeding the goals that you have set. When it comes to spending money, it cannot be outside of those lines. It cannot be a shot in the dark. You have to make sure that the money that you are spending is going to yield the return that you are looking for. When it comes to software, when it comes to building your team, when it comes to equipment, does it make sense to do it that particular way and with the price tag that is attached to it? Write this down somewhere that you will see daily: "Every trend is not your friend." Just because it's the latest and greatest does not mean that you need it for your business. Just because the hottest ticket out there right now is offering a workshop does not mean that it's going to help you. Be attached to your goals, both for your professional and personal life. Don't be attached to the next wave that decides to blow through. Your goals will help you navigate everything that presents itself to you.

We are bombarded with ads on social media every single day. They pop up on our computers when we're working, they pop up on our phones when we're listening to music. We cannot get away from them. One of the ways I filter through all of that noise is by reading the comments. Sometimes you've got to go through pages of comments because you don't know what's a real person and what's a BOT. Pay attention to people who are serving the same niche as you. Pay attention to the people who have been in business as long as you. Do your research on whatever they're offering. Don't just jump in and sign up because it's tickling your ears, tickling your fancy, or speaking to the area that you happen to be frustrated in at the time. The reality is, even when it's a great product, you may not yield a return for six to nine months. Can you pay that price tag and wait that long for a return? If not, then you need to go and find something that's comparable. I promise you that there are several products out there that are. They may not be running ads on social media, they may not be on the tip of everyone's tongue, but they are out there. Do yourself and your wallet a favor by doing your research, and make sure that it makes sense for the goals that you have established.

Strategy #4: You Cannot Free Your Way to Success

Stop giving everything away. Yes, you can do a free master class. Yes, you can have a free ebook. Yes, you can have a free hook item on your website. But if you keep giving away everything for free, how are you ever going to make money? At some point you have to believe in yourself and what you're offering. You have to know that what you're offering is the answer to somebody's problem. You have to know that the transformation you're offering is worth it. Be willing to step out and charge for what you're doing and what you're offering. When somebody comes up to you and wants to pick your brain, that's OK. There is a way to answer people's questions without giving them everything that you know. Nobody should be fully picking your brain for free. Understand that picking my brain comes with a price tag. For example, as a Simplified Productivity Coach, I offer a free strategy session on my website www.nichicamelton.com. Within that free strategy session, I offer my coaching services, which come at two levels. There is an a la carte and there is a four month program. Those who pay for my coaching program also get a copy of my book, because it will help in the coaching process. Then, periodically, there are emails that are sent out to everyone on my email list that gives them free nuggets. These nuggets are designed to attract those who are not in my coaching program and sustain those who are. That is a money generating and sustaining freebie.

Strategy #5. Know Your Worth

There are several people in business, whether they are newbies or seasoned, who truly do not know the value of the service or product they're offering. This is where doing research comes in. It is OK to Google people who do the same thing that you do, check out their website, and see what they're charging. It's also good to do some hands-on research when it's feasible. Does the quality match? Is it exactly the same product? What are the similarities and the differences? Find out what their sales are. Talk to them. Find out what the issues are that they've been having. How did they arrive at the price point that they're at right now? It doesn't have to be you who asks these questions. They don't have to know that you are the person looking. You can send somebody incognito. The point is to do your research.

You also need to know your demographic and what the people in your area that you serve are willing to pay. Are you brick and mortar or are you online or are you both? If you're online, then you obviously can reach people beyond your geographic location. However, if you are strictly brick and mortar and you strictly serve the people that are in your geographic location, then you have to pay attention to the demographic and you have to price accordingly. This means that you may need to change vendors. You may need to change where your brick and mortar is located. Is it easy for people to get to you by walking and riding the bus? Or are you so far out that a person has to have a car in order to get to your location? Do your hours match those of the people that you serve? If you're in an area where everybody is working a nine to five and you close at 6:00 pm every single day, are you giving your demographic the opportunity to get to you? All these things are critical factors in whether or not you will reach your financial goals. These are both money making and money sustaining activities that must take place within your business at least every six months. Why? Businesses are opening and closing every six months. You have to be ready to evaluate yourself and make the necessary adjustments so that you are amongst the ones that are in for the long haul.

The other side of this coin is that there are going to be people who are going to tell you that you are charging too much or charging too little. You have to pay attention to what your research shows you. For those that say that you are charging too much, ask yourself this question: Are they in my target market? If not, then their opinion doesn't matter. For the people who say you're not charging them enough, go back and look at your research. Did you read the research correctly? Did you evaluate it correctly? Are there new businesses in your area that you've missed? If you find that you reviewed the research correctly, then make minor changes such as putting out a tip jar. Then those who think that you're not charging enough have the free will to tip you the difference. Then both sides are happy. There are creative ways to meet both your financial goals and the needs of your niche market. Keep in mind you will have all kinds of customers, but you're paying attention to your target market. There will be people coming to your business or visiting your website who are outside of that target, and that's great; that means your reach is expanding. Always keep in mind that when you reevaluate your business, you need to evaluate your target market. Pay attention to who's coming in. Do surveys every now and then of the customers that are doing business with you. Make sure you are getting their contacts and their coins. There's a way for you to get their demographic information. Create an app that they scan every time they make a purchase. Sign new customers up in your system, so that every time they order you put in their phone number. Pay attention to the trends of your business and make the needed and necessary adjustments. A word of caution: Never, ever, ever make drastic changes. The drastic changes will drive your core, loyal customers away. Find out what your niche customer needs are and slowly integrate them in if they make sense for your overall goals.

Conclusion

Before you can create money making activities, you have to have money making and sustaining goals. If you have not done that for your business, it is time that you do it immediately. Then make sure the activities that you're doing on a daily basis are in alignment with your daily, weekly, and monthly goals. Do your research. Don't be afraid to ask yourself the hard questions. Get yourself a coach. As a matter of fact, you may have more than one, and that's fine. Some coaches, like myself, have programs that are only a few months long. Then you have other coaches who are there with you for years. You also need to get yourself a mentor. The combination of a coach and a mentor will help you ensure that your business reaches a level of success that you have only dreamed about.

To connect with me and sign up for your FREE strategy session, go to www.nichicamelton.com. As a Simplified Productivity Coach, I arm my clients with the necessary tools needed to improve their productivity by refining their scheduling and enhancing their organizational and prioritization skills. I am available to do the same for you. To help you see that what you have been dreaming about can become your reality.

Jessica Merritt

The Care Based Leadership Collaborative
President

www.linkedin.com/in/jessicaamerritt
https://www.facebook.com/JessicaSpradley/
https://www.instagram.com/jessica_spradley/
www.carebasedleadership.org
www.care-metrix.com

Dr. Jessica Merritt is the president and co-founder of The Care Based Leadership Collaborative, LLC. Dr. Merritt has over two decades of expert experience in educating others and specializes in diversity, equity, and inclusion (DEI). Her earned degrees include a Bachelor's and Master's degree in Sociology and a PhD in Social Foundations of Education with a specialty in Research and Measurement. In addition to her role at Care Based Leadership, LLC. Dr. Merritt has a demonstrated commitment to increasing the capacity for diversity, equity and inclusion in for-profit and non-profit organizations, K-12 districts, and higher education institutions through strategic planning, research, teaching, and curriculum design. Additionally, Dr. Merritt intentionally invests in the success of women through mentoring, coaching, and sponsorship to invest into the communities in which she, her daughters, and other women can thrive.

UNDERSTANDING AND OVERCOMING FINANCIAL FEAR: A DEEP DIVE

By Jessica Merritt

Financial fear is a complex and multifaceted emotion that affects a large part of the population, even across various socio-economic backgrounds. At its core, financial fear arises from the uncertainty associated with money, including the risk of losing financial stability, the anxiety over not having enough savings for retirement, or the dread of being overwhelmed by debt. This fear can manifest itself in many ways, influencing behavior and decision-making, often leading to a cycle of financial distress that, for many, has been passed down from generation to generation, creating a bond that can be challenging to break.

The Nature of Financial Fear

Financial fear can stem from a variety of sources. For some, it is rooted in their upbringing and the financial behaviors modeled by their parents or guardians. Those raised in households where money was a constant source of stress may develop a scarcity mindset, feeling perpetually that there is never enough money, regardless of their current financial status. For others, financial fear may arise from a traumatic event, such as a significant loss during a market crash, a sudden job loss, scarcity of needs being met because of money, or encountering large, unexpected expenses that took a toll on the family. Moreover, financial fear often thrives on a lack of knowledge. The financial world can seem intimidating with its jargon, complex products, and the ever-changing economic landscape. Without a solid understanding of financial principles, individuals may feel powerless and anxious about making decisions that could impact their financial health. While we are looking at understanding and overcoming financial fear and the resulting behaviors, it is important to also understand some potential psychological impacts on the individual and the others around them.

Psychological Impact of Financial Fear

The effects of financial anxiety extend well beyond simple stress about money. It can seriously undermine a person's mental health, leading to increased anxiety, depression, and a lowered sense of overall well-being. For example, someone constantly worried about meeting rent may experience debilitating anxiety, while another facing long-term debt might suffer from persistent depressive symptoms. Additionally, this type of stress can lead to physical symptoms such as insomnia, chronic headaches, and other conditions commonly associated with stress.

Financial fear can also influence behavior, causing some individuals to freeze up and make no decisions at all, or to act recklessly. For instance, a person overwhelmed by financial worry might completely ignore their financial responsibilities, like not opening bills or avoiding budgeting. On the other hand, another person might engage in risky financial behaviors such as compulsive shopping, gambling, or making high-risk investments to quickly solve their financial issues, often making their situation worse.

Social and Emotional Consequences

Financial fear can put significant pressure on personal relationships, as stress and anxiety about money affect interactions with partners, family members, and friends. Money is often a central issue in relationship conflicts, and financial instability can escalate these tensions. For example, a couple might argue more often about spending habits or financial priorities if they're facing economic hardships. Additionally, the embarrassment and stigma that often accompany financial difficulties may lead some individuals to withdraw socially. They might isolate themselves, pulling away from friendships and family ties that could provide essential emotional support and practical help.

Overcoming Financial Fear

While financial fear can be debilitating, it is not something that has to last forever. Overcoming this fear requires a proactive approach, focusing on education, planning, and emotional management.

1. Education: The first step in overcoming financial fear is to educate yourself about financial basics. Understanding how money works and learning about budgeting, savings, investments, and retirement planning can empower individuals and reduce anxiety. Many community organizations offer financial literacy workshops, and there are numerous resources available online and in libraries that can help build a solid foundation of financial knowledge.

2. Professional Help: For those who feel overwhelmed, seeking professional help can be a game-changer. Financial advisors can provide personalized advice tailored to individual financial situations, helping to develop strategies for knowledge development, debt management, savings, and investments. For those whose financial fear is rooted in deeper psychological issues, consulting with a financial therapist can be beneficial and a more practical next step. Professionals that specialize in helping individuals understand the emotional aspects of money and developing healthier financial behaviors can serve as a vital part of the healing process and a necessary part of the journey toward empowerment and success.

3. Strategic Financial Planning: Developing a financial plan can provide a sense of control and direction. This plan should include clear, achievable goals, such as paying off debt, saving

a certain amount of money on a consistent basis, or investing for retirement. Monitoring progress toward these goals can provide reassurance of decision making, hope for sustained change, and can motivate further action.

4. Building a Support Network: Sharing financial fears and goals with trusted friends or family members can alleviate the feeling of isolation and provide much-needed support and accountability. There is an element of vulnerability that is needed so the environment must be safe, but if you have the opportunity, please share and be honest with a family member or close friend who can support you along the journey.

Financial fear is a powerful emotion that can significantly impact one's quality of life and financial stability. However, by understanding its roots, addressing the associated emotional and psychological challenges, and taking proactive steps toward financial literacy and planning, individuals can transform their fear into an opportunity for growth and security. The journey to overcoming financial fear is not only about managing money, but also about gaining confidence and achieving a more stable, fulfilling life.

Financial Landscape in the Black Community

In my personal experience with navigating financial fear and moving toward empowerment, I realized that racial identity was a factor that impacted my experience. As a Black woman, I understand that my experience is different from many others'. The financial landscape within the Black community in the United States is a complex tapestry woven with historical, social, and economic threads. Each thread represents various aspects of life that have shaped the financial experiences and outcomes for Black Americans over the years. From the legacy of systemic inequalities and discrimination to the vibrant tales of resilience and success, understanding finances in the Black community requires a dive into past and present factors that influence economic experiences.

Historical Overview

The financial history of Black Americans cannot be separated from the history of racial discrimination in the U.S. From slavery to the Jim Crow era to modern systemic biases, these historical realities have had long-lasting effects on economic opportunities for Black individuals. Post-slavery, the denial of the ability to own land or accumulate wealth continued through discriminatory practices such as redlining and the denial of GI Bill benefits to Black veterans. These are just a few of the historical practices which have contributed to current disparities in wealth.

Current Financial Realities

As of today, the wealth gap between Black families and non-black families is still significant. According to data from the Federal Reserve's Survey of Consumer Finances, the typical white family has eight times the wealth of the typical Black family. This disparity is evident in various financial metrics:

Homeownership: Homeownership is a critical means of building wealth in America. However, Black homeownership rates are significantly lower compared to their white counterparts. Factors contributing to this include lower incomes, higher loan denial rates, and a historic lack of inherited wealth, which affects down payment capabilities.

Income Inequality: Black workers face wage disparities that persist despite educational attainment. Discriminatory hiring practices, lower access to high-paying jobs, and segregation in low-wage sectors are some of the systemic barriers that maintain income inequality.

Education and Student Debt: Higher education is often seen as a pathway to economic mobility, but it comes at a high cost. Black college students are more likely to take on student debt, and the burden of this debt is heavier on average than that of their white peers, affecting their financial stability long after graduation.

Retirement Savings: The disparities in income and savings rates also extend to retirement planning. Black Americans are less likely to have private retirement accounts or pension funds, partly due to lower rates of access to these benefits at work.

Efforts Toward Economic Empowerment

Despite these challenges, there is a strong movement toward economic empowerment and resilience within the Black community. Several strategies and initiatives have been adopted both within and outside the community to enhance financial literacy and independence:

Community Banking: Black-owned banks and credit unions play a crucial role in providing fair financial services and supporting economic development within Black communities. These institutions often focus on community-building and provide loans to small businesses and individuals who might otherwise be denied by larger banks.

Entrepreneurship: There is a growing trend of entrepreneurship in the Black community as a way to build wealth and create jobs. Black entrepreneurs are starting businesses at a fast rate, particularly Black women. However, access to capital remains a significant hurdle due to disparities in wealth and difficulties in securing loans.

Financial Education and Literacy Programs: Nonprofits, community groups, and even some financial institutions offer programs designed to increase financial literacy in the Black community. These programs teach basic financial skills, including budgeting, saving, investing, and understanding credit, which are essential for making informed financial decisions.

Policy Advocacy: Advocacy for policy changes that directly address economic disparities is crucial. This includes advocating for fair lending practices, equitable funding for schools, reforms in housing policies, and improved access to healthcare, all of which impact financial health.

Social Investments: There is an increasing focus on social investments that support community services, affordable housing projects, and local enterprises. These investments not only provide financial returns but also contribute to the economic and social well-being of Black communities.

Future Outlook

The road to financial equity is long and fraught with challenges, but the resilience and proactive efforts of the Black community continue to foster hope. The increasing visibility of Black financial issues has sparked broader public and private sector interest in addressing and supporting economic equality efforts. With continued advocacy, education, and community empowerment, there can be significant strides toward closing the financial disparities and relieving the debilitating manifestations of financial fear faced by Black Americans.

The financial landscape in the United States is shaped by a unique combination of challenges and opportunities. The impact of history, financial challenges that continue over generations, and financial fear has for too long paralyzed people into a stagnant place. Let's explore some examples of women who have overcome these challenges.

A Case Study

I remember the first time I was offered a credit card application. It was my first year of college and I was terrified of life. My mom had just left me days prior, and I was on my own. I was only 17 years old…and I was on my own. I remember being at the resource fair and being summoned over by a calming voice explaining that all I needed to do was fill out this short application and I would receive an invite to a reception with food and get a free t-shirt. He had me at free t-shirt! I filled out the application and about two weeks later I got the card in the mail. Excited is an understatement. I just got paid $3500!

For those who understand credit cards, you know that I didn't get paid $3500. At that time, I didn't understand the concept of credit, so I thought it was free money. You can imagine how the spending story goes…but the payback story had a lasting impact. It took me five years to pay back too many trips to big box stores and food delivery orders. Those years included late payments, missed payments, collection calls, negotiations, ignoring calls, and everything in between. In short, it was a journey that created so much anxiety that I had anxiety around financial decisions well into adulthood. I was convinced that I had made the wrong decision before, and I didn't want to do it again.

Financial fear is a pervasive barrier that can stifle ambition and curtail financial growth. My fear had me frozen financially. Over the past decade, I cannot count the women who have expressed some sort of negative experience, or dare I say traumatic experience, around finances that caused a freeze response that made even exploring financial literacy a daunting task. This experience, the stories of other women, and my desired level of comfort with finances for my daughters drive the passion about overcoming financial fears and empowering individuals, especially women, to achieve financial independence and literacy. This passion reflects a dedication to demystifying the complexities of personal finance and investment, addressing both the psychological and practical aspects of managing money.

One of the primary problems we need to address is the fear around money, which often leads to poor financial decisions or prevents individuals from making any decisions at all. We need to make it a conversation and not a judgment call. By tackling the emotional and psychological barriers associated with money—such as fear of debt, anxiety around investments, and a scarcity mindset—we can highlight a pathway to knowledge and release some of the constraints by creating proactive financial management options. This chapter delves into a few of the mental hurdles that often cloud financial judgment and hinder effective decision-making. It is important to name, discuss, and address barriers to financial literacy. Through the narratives of three women who conquered their fears, we explore the transformative journey from financial anxiety to empowerment. These stories not only serve as a beacon of hope but also offer practical strategies that can be applied to dismantle financial fears and build a robust financial future.

Emma's Journey from Debt to Wealth

Emma's story began in the shadow of substantial credit card debt. Having grown up in a middle-class family where discussing money was taboo, Emma entered adulthood with little financial literacy. Her early career in graphic design provided her enough income to explore her independence, which unfortunately translated into unchecked spending and poor financial decisions. The turning point came when Emma faced the possibility of bankruptcy. The fear of hitting rock bottom was palpable. However, instead of allowing her situation to define her, Emma chose to redefine her relationship with money.

Emma's first step was acknowledging her fear of financial ruin. She started by educating herself about personal finance, reading books, attending workshops, and following financial advisors online. This self-education was her weapon against fear, transforming it from a paralyzing force into a motivating factor. Emma's approach to overcoming her debt was methodical. She adopted the snowball method, where she paid off smaller debts first, gaining momentum as each balance was cleared. Additionally, she began tracking her spending meticulously, cutting non-essential expenses, and setting strict budgets for herself. Over five years, Emma not only cleared her debt but also started investing in stocks and mutual funds. Her journey from a fearful spender to a savvy investor exemplifies how understanding and navigating one's fears can lead to profound financial transformation.

Linda's Battle with Investment Anxiety

Linda, a successful real estate agent, had always been apprehensive of the stock market. Her anxiety stemmed from a deep-seated fear of losing money, influenced by her family's conservative financial approaches and a volatile market crash she witnessed in her early twenties. Despite her success in real estate, Linda's portfolio lacked diversification, which is essential for mitigating risk and enhancing potential returns. Her fear of investment losses kept her from exploring other lucrative avenues.

The catalyst for change was meeting a financial mentor who specialized in investments. This mentorship was crucial in helping Linda understand the nature of market fluctuations and the long-term benefits of a diversified portfolio. Linda started with low-risk investments, such as bonds and index funds, to acclimate herself to the market's dynamics. As her confidence grew, she diversified into stocks, real estate investment trusts (REITs), and eventually, international markets. Through gradual engagement and continuous learning, Linda overcame her investment anxiety. Her portfolio's growth enhanced her financial stability and broadened her understanding of wealth accumulation strategies.

Sarah's Escape from the Scarcity Mindset

Sarah's financial outlook was dominated by a scarcity mindset, rooted in her childhood experiences of poverty. This fear manifested in extreme frugality, preventing her from enjoying the fruits of her labor and from investing in her future.

The journey to financial liberation began with Sarah confronting her past. She sought the help of a financial therapist to address the psychological roots of her scarcity mindset. This therapeutic approach helped her realize that her spending fears were deeply intertwined with her fear of reverting to poverty. Armed with a new perspective, Sarah started to loosen her stringent hold on her finances. She allocated funds for personal development, such as education and health, which she had previously deemed unnecessary expenditures. Moreover, she began contributing to a retirement plan and an emergency fund, which bolstered her financial security and alleviated her fears of financial instability.

Emma, Linda, and Sarah's stories illuminate the path from fear to financial empowerment. By confronting their financial fears, educating themselves, and implementing tailored strategies, they were able to transform their anxieties into opportunities for growth and success.

Conclusion

This chapter underscores the importance of facing financial fears head-on. Whether it's the fear of debt, the anxiety of investment, or the dread of poverty, recognizing and overcoming these fears is crucial for anyone aiming to achieve financial independence and success. Through education, strategy, and sometimes professional help, financial fears can be converted into steps toward a secure and prosperous financial future.

Tanya Kravcenko

Chartered Accountant, Author

https://www.linkedin.com/company/tanyakravcenko/
https://www.facebook.com/TheJellybeanTheory
https://www.instagram.com/tanyakravcenkonz/
www.tanyakravcenko.com

Tanya Kravcenko is a chartered accountant with a passion for financial literacy and has more than 20 years of industry experience. After spending her career supporting small businesses and entrepreneurs, Tanya noticed a significant gap in financial literacy among younger (and even older) generations. This inspired her to develop coaching sessions to empower people with the tools to make positive life choices and reach their full potential.

YOU ARE YOUR BRAND

By Tanya Kravcenko

The first time I heard this I thought, What does that mean? How am I a product?

Since I was a teenager I have always been intrigued by the business world. I studied accounting in high school as well as shorthand/typing, thinking that shorthand would be an asset as it was a quick way to write. Little did I know back in 1984 what technology would provide for us in the future. I wanted to go to university, but my father said there was no point as I would just get married and have children. Yes, I did want children, but I also enjoyed learning, so I decided not to listen to my father's words and did both. I got my degree and got to be a mother.

My father's words were an expression of how men thought in 1984. My mother chose to give up her career of choice to look after her family. My mother did not come of age in an era during which contraception was available. I was so lucky I had a choice when and if I wanted to have a child. This was the most liberating invention for women. So, who were my business role models? I had no family members or friends of my parents who had chosen to be an entrepreneur. I guess it was just in my DNA from the beginning. My father had owned his own businesses during my childhood, but he was unsuccessful due to a lack of financial literacy and personal challenges.

Throughout my working career in a male dominated arena, I experienced the same mindset my father had from my employers— women were thought of as breeding factories and not as equals in the workplace. When I graduated, I saw more women than men graduating in business and law. The women also made the top marks. That is when I knew I was on the right track and knew women could be successful in the business arena too. Opportunities were given to me in leading roles, but I was never given the ultimate position. It was always a male.

When I reflect on my mindset back then, I realize that I thought I was a woman who had two roles to play in life. My first role was to be a mother and not to feel guilty that I also wanted to pursue my career as a chartered accountant. That is why I started my first business in public practice. I wanted to be available to my daughter and share all the special moments in her life but also be available to my clients. For 10 years my public practice served both me and my daughter, but it wasn't enough. I had witnessed clients who owned companies but had an employee mindset. They thought if they worked more hours they would make more money. I learned at a very young age when my father died when I was 21 that time is the limiting factor in life. So, work smart, not hard. I also noticed my clients could not understand their financial statements. To be in business you need to know your numbers. That is when I created my new brand and product and am now a financial literacy and mindset coach. I am also an author and have written two books on this topic.

I learned that to be a successful entrepreneur, although you may be an expert at your trade, if you do not understand how money works and how to read your financial statements you will find it hard work. I also learned that a business plan is the first thing you should complete before you start a business. When I was creating my new brand, I spent three hours with my business coach discussing what I wanted my ultimate business to be and finding my why. Every big successful company I had worked for had a mission statement. But I found that if this was not followed by the leaders at the top of the company then it meant nothing. My coach taught me, once you know your "why," everything you do in your business should align with it. My coach asked me what I liked doing and then three words summed up my "why"—teaching financial success. Everything I do through my brand aligns with those three words. It also summed up who I was as a person and what I wanted to do with my clients whilst in public practice, but it frustrated me as the clients did not have the financial literacy training. That is when I wrote a letter to the prime minister advising her that financial literacy in New Zealand is in a poor state and it needs to change. I also noticed when my daughter was learning math at school that she did not understand the concept of the value of a number, and I sought external coaching for her. That was the best decision I made for her at the age of six. The coach was a retired teacher, and she knew that numbers are also patterns. As my daughter is quite artistic, she understood her teaching methods straight away and I saw her maths comprehension improve dramatically—to the point that other parents wanted to set up after-school lessons with our teacher.

If you learn the value of a number when you are young, you will understand this concept as an adult. While in practice I also noticed most of my clients did not have a budget that they stuck to. I was gifted with a memory that could remember numbers. I always carry my personal budget around with me in my head. Now I am creating a user-friendly budget model. This tool will also include a time budget. As this is the limiting factor in our lives, this is what I will complete first with my clients going forward. Once you know what you want to complete in your lifetime the money will come. Setting goals and a timeframe is the first thing you should do. Your personal life is also a business as it is dictated by the two main factors in life—time and money. The third factor that is required in any business/life plan is the mindset. This is more important now than anything else. The world we live in is at a faster pace than our forefathers. The role of a woman has changed dramatically. When my mum was a school leaver her opportunities were limited. If she got pregnant when she was young ie before the age of 25 as most women did, then her destiny was to carry on having babies. No daycare was available, so the mother's role was to stay at home and be the caregiver. Now women can go to work, give the caregiving role to a paid entity and enjoy the financial rewards. But then women started to miss out on the "play" part of life. I learned a lot about myself and my daughter by being a stay-at-home mum and getting lots of opportunities to play with her.

Women then joined the gym to keep fit, got massages and beauty treatments to feel good about our image, socialised in bars and cafes rather than at home (maybe so we did not have to do the cleaning afterwards or we did not have time to do some home baking as our mothers did). We also had the opportunity to delegate tasks like cleaning and to hire a cleaner. We paid for our cars to be valeted. Solo mothers could hire someone to mow our lawns and maintain our gardens as we became time poor. Now that 50% of marriages are unsuccessful the outsourcing of support has grown. While I was running my accounting practice and owned a seven-acre property as a solo mother I was lucky to have supportive female friends who could assist my daughter with her horse-riding passion. I also swapped grazing for the expertise of a father to maintain our property. I created a village on my property where five young girls could graze their horses and my daughter could have other like-minded people around her to support her interest. Their parents would share their knowledge of horses and share equipment so the girls could go to their horse-riding competitions. None of us were super wealthy but by sharing what we had helped our children be the best riders that they could be, and they just loved coming home with the different coloured ribbons and cups.

All my life I have surrounded myself with a village that has uplifted me and assisted me to where I want to be. My longest friend, Ann, who I met when I was seven years old, has always believed in everything I have tried to achieve and has been there to support me. We both came from parents who were not asset-rich but life-rich. We both grew up in an area where money was not a surplus but had parents who showed us anything is possible if you put your mind to it and the rewards are worth it. Our parents also taught us without us knowing that we are our brand. What we do, how we present ourselves and what we provide is our brand. Quite often Ann and I will chat about our careers and how we get frustrated with people who accept low standards. We'll laugh and say that we don't do average. My father also had a saying: "You do it once and you do it right." Due to this I found it hard to accept when I did something wrong but over the years I have learned that it is the mistakes that teach you the biggest lessons.

The biggest lesson I learned in my career is to surround yourself with other like-minded people. There is always something to learn. When I was in public practice, I joined a networking group called Venus where women would come together fortnightly to tell everyone in a minute who they were and what their business was and what they were looking for. Then we would discuss our wins. It was always great to see how other women had risen above the challenges of the previous fortnight and had a successful outcome. But the best thing about this networking group was that every fortnight it was a requisite for each of us to meet with two other women and this is where the magic would happen. As we got to know each other the trust would build and so would our businesses. At the end of each meeting, we would ask each other, "What can I do to help you?" This was something I found hard to answer as I had always been the helper. Once I learned how to answer the question, my business grew, and I grew as a person. I realised it was okay to ask for help.

In other networking groups I had been a member of, the largest part of the "why" for the group was to grow income, i.e. be each other's salespeople. This did not align with my values and beliefs, as I saw that in business if you had a good product or service and a good relationship with your customers your business would naturally grow. People put trust in you (your brand) more than anything. Everyone wants to know who the founder of a company is, and what they do in their business and personal life. Moreso now people want to know what companies are doing to make the world a better place—what their workplace ethics are, do staff have the opportunity for a balanced lifestyle, are they paid adequately, is there support for their mindset. What practices are put in place to reduce waste and pollution. These topics were never printed on a set of financial statements when I first started studying my degree. Now it is the first thing people want to look at. People are making their purchasing choices based on non-financial information; sometimes price does not matter.

Throughout my career as a boss and employer I have always worked with people who supported me as a team. We all had the same goal no matter what level you were at in the team. When I shared my values and beliefs with my team members, they always gave me their full commitment and respect. I also had a winning team that got the job done and had a happy environment at the same time. When I closed my accounting practice in January 2023, I found it difficult to say goodbye to my clients because they had been part of my team for ten years. They had contributed to making me who I am today and also provided me with an income and lifestyle so that I could be the mother/person I wanted to be. These values came from my upbringing which again I took for granted. It was not until I wrote my first book and shared it with an elite business owner at my high school that I realised I was lucky to have parents and role models when I grew up who always treated our family like a team. We all had jobs, we all helped each other, and we always had fun. The money was not the most important thing in life. My mother and father did work hard to earn it, but they also knew how to share it and use it to get the best life for their five children and our grandfather who was also living with us.

When I was asked to teach a class of thirty 16-18-year olds about financial literacy, I felt very honoured to stand in the front of the classroom where I had once sat. The pupils were very attentive for three hours and listened to what I had learned since I left Manurewa High School. I showed them you can do it yourself if you really want to. You can listen to the negative comments if you want to. Or you can build a village around yourself and do what our school motto said: "Aim High." That day was the most moving day of my life. I came away knowing I had found my destiny. This is what I was meant to do my whole life. During my career I had worked in teaching roles, travelling around New Zealand teaching clients how to use the tax software we developed. What I didn't know at the time was that thirty years later I would be teaching financial literacy around the world through online programs. In 1990 emails were the best invention for business and people were still embracing the ease of communication. Keeping up with change in the electronic world is our biggest challenge today. When I ran my practice, the software for Xero and MYOB was changing constantly. So were the tax legislation and legal rules. Keeping up with all the changes during COVID was one of the most challenging things for me and my clients. Our prime minister was constantly changing the tax rules and it made it very difficult for both me and my client to apply them. Some of the rule changes I found destructive for some industries. I have a close relationship with the current minister of small businesses and have expressed my concerns. I could see that our prime minister Jacinda Adern was not financially literate and did not understand the impact of her decisions. Now our country is recovering from them, and a new government is trying to rectify the damage. When a country has a leader that is financially literate, that is when we are the most successful.

In this decade I have noticed more than ever that women are eager to set up their small businesses so they can have work-life balance while also doing what they love at the same time and earning an income to sustain their lifestyle. When I became a solo mother, I had financial discussions with women at a depth I had never experienced before, from women who lived day to day and wanted to know how to improve their cash flow to women who were multimillionaires and did not know what to do with their money if their husbands died.

As part of my brand awareness campaign, I ran an evening session called "Financial Awareness for Women" in a local pub owned by a woman who ran a Pink Ladies group that met once a month. I invited a financial advisor, an insurance specialist and a lawyer to the event to speak about topics affecting women. The information that was shared was just what the ladies wanted to hear. The look on some of the women's faces after the presentations were ones of concern as a lot of the women in the room were not financially literate and left the money decisions up to their husbands. A few of the women in the room were in blended marriages which brought up a lot of questions when the lawyer spoke (he got a lot of business that night). The insurance specialist spoke about income protection and how that is our biggest asset, yet we do not think to insure against the loss of it. He got a lot of business that night, too. The biggest thing I learned that night is how fearful people are of being put in charge of money. The negative attitude towards money was very evident in the room. I feel we have made the world way more complicated than it needs to be when it comes to money. Money should be a positive subject and should be thought of in abundance. I have had this attitude my whole life. Again, I just thought it was normal when I won a share of first division lotto when I was 25 when I asked the universe for a solution to a loan repayment. It did not bother me as I put all the winnings into my first house. I always treated money as a way to happiness no matter how big or small the sum was. When I was a solo mother on several occasions, I had to be creative to find solutions for money situations. Always a solution would arise, and it was usually by swapping resources. Recently I experienced swapping a meal in a fast-food place for a copy of my book. Back in the old days, swapping of services/products was commonly used. The barter card started this concept again and now we have crypto currency.

When I was young my father taught me how to barter. He came from Yugoslavia, where it was a common custom. When I watched him as a child at the local markets, people would frown at him when he would discount the price. As an adult I go into businesses and when they present the bill, I ask them with a smile on my face if they have a sunny day discount. It is on sunny days I do this. Every time the owner will say sure. Now my friends try this way of bartering with success too. What I have also learned from this process is to believe in your worth. I grew up watching my parents perform a lot of acts of service for family and friends without asking for monetary compensation. My parents were cash-poor and love-rich. I started my accounting practice this way but learned very quickly that this would not serve me for very long. Thankfully a very clever accounting colleague advised me not to devalue the accounting brand and charge my worth. I had to put aside my personal feelings for my clients and put on my business hat when it came to invoicing time. If the invoice was too much for my client at the time I would arrange a repayment plan and 100% of the time I got full payment for my invoice. This also taught me that the money will come—sometimes it just takes longer than the due date. The important lesson was that I kept that client for ten years and therefore did not have to build a relationship with a new one.

Whilst working in a male dominated arena I learned one major difference and that is that we do think differently when it comes to finding solutions. The female side of the brain is very much about nurture and growth whereas the male side of the brain is about hunting and gathering. Recently it was pointed out to me how I can use both male and female attitudes when it comes to problem solving. Growing up with three brothers and a father, our house was predominantly driven by males. My mother was very black and white, and system driven which worked in her favour with the number of people in the household and the income that was provided to support us. These were amazing skills I picked up and were my first financial literacy lessons in life. Money may be scarce, but it is what you do with it that matters. My father could be impulsive, but my mother was budget driven and therefore all bills were paid on time and their credit rating was always protected.

When I would attend business meetings, I was gifted with the ability to read a room very quickly and to understand the issues that needed to be addressed and how to find a simple solution. Again, another technique my mother taught me. She was always able to pivot when it came to money solutions. It was not easy, but it was possible. This is the approach I had when times were tough in any business situation. Once my boss commented that he could not believe how I did it sometimes. The days of cutting coupons with my mum and watching her allocate the cash from dads pay packet each week paid off. Once a psychologist told me that I was very good at putting problems into boxes and addressing each one when necessary. This worked well for my mindset. It helped me in those times when I was feeling overwhelmed and would recall the phrase, "How does a lion eat an elephant? One bite at a time."

In business meetings I could see where people were talking via their ego rather than telling the truth. I would not be shy to diplomatically call them out on it. Sometimes my actions would backfire on me, but they were always with the best intentions. When I was in practice, I saw a lot of egos in action, especially when I was given a new client and the previous accountant had not done a professional job. When I would try to discuss the error and how we could fix it with the least impact on the client, they would usually not want to participate in the solution. Admitting you are wrong is one of the hardest things to do but once it has been done the solution can be found. Growing up in a family of five children who were competitive and openly critical was good practice for this skillset. It gave me the confidence to be open and honest in tense situations. Recently my mother passed away and one thing I asked her was if she had any regrets. Her answer was no. She was happy with the life she had lived, and she wouldn't have changed a thing.

To be true to yourself is the best thing you can do. To live a life you love is also very important. To chase the money only serves you if you are doing what you love otherwise it becomes a chore. Over the last year I have earned no money, but have become very rich as I have been true to myself and am living my dream: to teach financial success and share the lessons I have learned. The money will come in perfect timing as it always does.

Women do understand women. This is why we need to support each other and help each other keep our crowns on. When I was at Playcentre with my daughter, I put my hand up to be one of the leaders who could open each session. I would not have been able to be a leader if one of the other mums did not assist me with watching my child as she played on sessions while I was at other Playcentres being trained in how to be a leader. The skills I learned at playcentre are invaluable and one of the most important ones was the importance of learning through play. I will carry this attitude into my new brand. My recent book, *Charlie the Cyclist*, is aimed at eight year olds and teaches financial literacy in a fun way while also teaching Charlie how to make his own little business plan so he can buy the bike he needs to win a race. It is only 24 pages long. At Manurewa High School when I discussed goal setting it took five adults to assist the thirty pupils so they could understand the concept of goal setting. Again, a tool I learned from my parents who regularly set goals and had a plan in place for how to achieve them. By working together all goals were met.

As a world, we need to apply this team approach. There is no need for wars, poverty, young children dying from malnutrition etc. If we all worked together as a team, the world would be full of love and peace. This is my goal going forward. I have created a brand called Wahine loving Wahine which is Maori for Women loving Women, and wherever we go we do things to support each other. One day a lady walked into a café and I thought, I want to buy her a coffee. It was my good deed for the day. When she sat with me to drink it and talk about her job, I was so appreciative when she offered to help my business by providing a space where I can teach financial literacy. She also loved my brand Wahine loving Wahine. I knew she was a Maori because she had a moko on her chin which is worn by women who have an elite status.

I was taught hands are for helping not hurting. I would like to throw away all guns that are used for killing people, remove all boundaries stopping people from having the basic necessities in life which are food, clothing, shelter and medicine.

Currently I am creating my financial literacy school called SOL – School of Life. It incorporates all the things you need to know in life to survive – cooking, clothing and shelter and will teach financial literacy in all these areas in a practical way. If you incorporate it in everyday life you will learn in a fun way! It will be opening in June and I look forward to sharing it with you.

In my experience, when I have been developing my brand I have looked for perfection. Recently I learned that it does not exist. Everything in life is beautiful just the way it is. It is not broken and does not need to be fixed. Once I overcame this mindset, the creativity inside me flowed abundantly. I showed up as a person I never knew existed. My healer could see it and other people in my life could too, but I was always looking for perfection. This held me back in so many ways and now I am free from that way of thinking.

Recently I became an author in an international best seller. It was my dream to have a brand that was recognised around the world, and it happened so easily. I achieved that with a company that sees only beauty and understands the importance of collaboration and love and lifting each other up. Their brand makes things simple and easy to use. Within a month an anthology was created with 15 authors around the world. The owner of the company believed it would be an international bestseller and had faith that all of us would be able to make it happen. The biggest lesson here for me is that when you believe in yourself and surround yourself with a village who does too, magic happens!

I doubted that I would be able to achieve this status, but a very intelligent man confirmed for me that I am an authority in my field and pointed out that the first six letters spell "author." How ironic is that?

Now it is time for me to accept the recognition and turn it into a possibility for other people so they can make their dreams come true. I will do this by writing programmes for my financial literacy school that are simple and practical just like She Rises Studios has done.

I wish to thank She Rises Studios for allowing me to share my journey with them and also for introducing me to so many kind and loving people. The most important currency is love, and you cannot put a price on it.

JOIN THE MOVEMENT!
#BAUW

Becoming An Unstoppable Woman
With She Rises Studios

She Rises Studios was founded by Hanna Olivas and Adriana Luna Carlos, the mother-daughter duo, in mid-2020 as they saw a need to help empower women worldwide. They are the podcast hosts of the *She Rises Studios Podcast* and Amazon best-selling authors and motivational speakers who travel the world. Hanna and Adriana are the movement creators of #BAUW - Becoming An Unstoppable Woman: The movement has been created to universally impact women of all ages, at whatever stage of life, to overcome insecurities, and adversities, and develop an unstoppable mindset. She Rises Studios educates, celebrates, and empowers women globally.

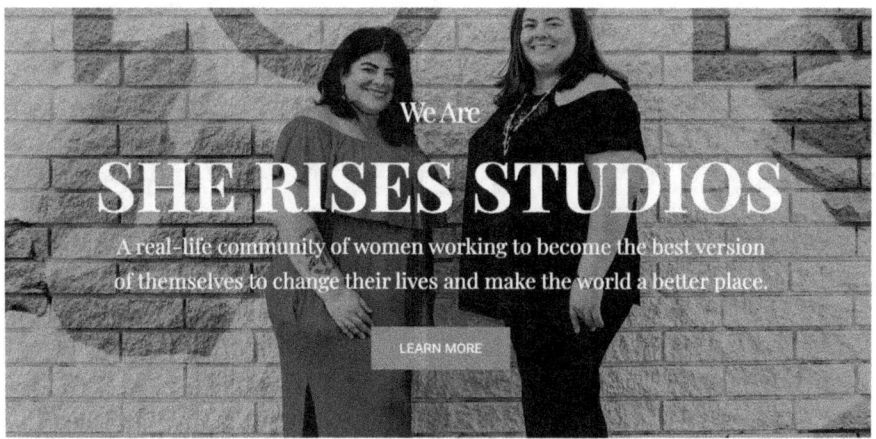

Looking to Join Us in our Next Anthology

or Publish YOUR Own?

She Rises Studios Publishing offers full-service publishing, marketing, book tour, and campaign services. For more information,

contact info@sherisesstudios.com

We are always looking for women who want to share their stories and expertise and feature their businesses on our podcasts, in our books, and in our magazines.

SEE WHAT WE DO

OUR PODCAST   **OUR BOOKS**   **OUR SERVICES**

Be featured in the Becoming An Unstoppable Woman magazine, published in 13 countries and sold in all major retailers. Get the visibility you need to LEVEL UP in your business!

Have your own TV show streamed across major platforms like

Roku TV, Amazon Fire Stick, Apple TV and more!

Learn to leverage your expertise. Build your online presence and grow your audience with FENIX TV.

https://fenixtv.sherisesstudios.com/

Visit www.SheRisesStudios.com to see how YOU can join the #BAUW movement and help your community to achieve the UNSTOPPABLE mindset.

Have you checked out the *She Rises Studios Podcast?*

Find us on all MAJOR platforms: Spotify, IHeartRadio,

Apple Podcasts, Google Podcasts, etc.

Looking to become a sponsor or build a partnership?

Email us at info@sherisesstudios.com

www.ingramcontent.com/pod-product-compliance
Lightning Source LLC
Chambersburg PA
CBHW071408120626
46546CB00002B/858